SCAR TISSUE

SCAR TISSUE by Melissa Dlugoleck
Published by IG Introspections, an imprint of Inspired Girl Publishing Group, a division of Inspired Girl Enterprises
Asbury Park, NJ 07712
inspiredgirlbooks.com

Inspired Girl Publishing Group is honored to bring forth books with heart and stories that matter. We are proud to offer this book to our readers; the story, the experiences, and the words are the author's alone. The stories portrayed within Scar Tissue are based on actual events. In some incidents, characteristics, names, and timelines may have been compressed or combined to protect the privacy and preserve the anonymity of people involved. The conversations in the book all come from the author's recollections, though they are not written to represent word-for-word transcripts.

This book is written as a source of information only. The information contained in this book should by no means be considered a substitute for the advice of a qualified medical professional. In addition, the publisher and the author assume no responsibility for errors, inaccuracies, omissions, or any other inconsistencies herein. The use of this book implies your acceptance of this disclaimer. Products, books, trademarks, and trademark names are used throughout this book to describe and inform the reader about various proprietary products that are owned by third parties. No endorsement of the information contained in this book is given by the owners of such products and trademarks, and no endorsement is implied by the inclusion of products, books, or trademarks in this book.

ISBN: 978-1-965240-23-6
Written by: Melissa Dlugolecki
Editorial & Creative Director: Jenn Tuma-Young
Lead Designer: Andrej Semnic
Book Editing, Packaging, and Production: Inspired Girl Publishing Group
Library of Congress Control Number: 2025945468

SCAR TISSUE

How to find relief from the pain of your emotional wounds without toxic positivity

MELISSA DLUGOLECKI

FOREWORD BY ERIK ROCK

I did something I never thought I would do.

A ceremony, to release my grief.

To set Leyden's soul free.

So that she can do her soul's work.

Something I definitely didn't imagine partaking in when I booked my trip to Tulum.

My intention was based in the belief that if Leyden is worried about watching over me, she can't fully elevate to what she needs to do, for her.

I know that not everyone will resonate with this, and I honor that.

In fact, up until the last year or so, I wouldn't have, either.

But this is where I am on my journey.

And it felt really important, really hard, and really loving

To set her soul free.

I made a commitment to instead of asking Leyden to help me or take care of me…

To reassure her that I am OK.

Encourage her to do what she needs to do.

And thank her for all of her love.

In a weird way, it added a layer of grieving, to my grief.

My healer's intention was to help me set my soul free.

He said that it would open up space for me to give all the love I have within me, not just in honoring Leyden, but to people here on this earth, who need me now.

Whether it's loss of life, a relationship, a job, a "normal" holiday season or the way you envisioned your life to be, there are layers of grief lurking in all of it.

I have learned from Leyden and this journey, that releasing is actually one of the most loving things we can do for others, and ourselves, too.

Even if it hurts.

CONTENTS

Contents

To my sweet, stubborn, and strong daughter Leyden; my greatest teacher.

*Thank you for choosing me to be your
mom. You taught me the beauty, the
burn, and the boundlessness of love.*

*You are in every page, every word, every
breath of this book.*

*Thank you for making me brave enough
to live with an open heart again.*

*For teaching me I am entitled to
nothing, but worthy of everything.*

This is for you.

*And to every person who's had to piece
together a life after loss, or walk a path
of plan "b" when plan "a" didn't go as
desired…this book is for you, too.*

You don't have to carry it alone.

Shine on baby girl, shine on.

Foreword

BY ERIK ROCK

There are moments in life that split you in half. Moments that don't just break your heart...they take your soul, your sense of self, your identity, your meaning, and everything you once believed was safe in the world.

That's what grief does. And if you've ever felt it...you know. It's the thing we dread the most. You know what it feels like to be alive and dead at the same time. To be surrounded by people but feel completely alone. To go through the motions while your soul stays buried under the weight of a silent scream. For most people, grief becomes a life sentence.

It enslaves them quietly, locking their potential in a prison of pain. It steals their voice, their energy, their dream...until they're just going through the motions, pretending they're okay while silently drowning inside.

Most people don't come back from that place. But my friend Melissa did. And the way she came back? It was nothing short of a resurrection.

I first hired Melissa to help me take my brand online...just a simple, three-month contract. I thought I was getting a strategist. A pro. A sharp mind to help build systems and scale reach.

What I didn't expect was that I was hiring a powerhouse human with so much impact potential trapped inside her heart. A mission inside her teaming to explode to the world. A woman who would not only transform the trajectory of my brand...but forever shift the way I see grief, healing, purpose, and power.

What started as a short-term agreement is now years of collaboration, growth, trust, creation, countless hours of strategy, real breakthroughs, and a level of impact I couldn't have done without her. But more than anything, it became a powerful connection rooted in something much deeper than business.

Because once I heard her story...the real story...the tragic, shattering, gut-wrenching truth of what she lived through...everything clicked.

The moment she told me about losing her daughter Leyden...

The moment I felt the weight of that pain through her words...

The moment I realized what she had survived...

It was like every part of me sat still and listened.

That was the moment I truly saw her.

You don't walk through that kind of fire and come out the same.

Melissa had been through hell...and not only did she rise from the ashes, she brought power back with her.

Suddenly, everything about her made sense. Her relentless work ethic. Her intuitive brilliance. Her deep presence. Her commitment to excellence. The way she shows up for people with this full-hearted intensity that says: "You matter. I see you. You're not alone." Constantly putting others before herself. Always ready to deliver value and serve.

This wasn't just talent. This was mission. Underneath her strategy, her coaching, her creativity...was a deep, undeniable fire. Her work doesn't come from theory. It comes from battle. It comes from having her heart shattered into dust...and choosing, day after day, to gather the pieces and build something that could help others heal.

Melissa's presence is electric. Her capacity to serve is unmatched. And the wisdom she carries? It's born from SCAR TISSUE...not textbooks. She has taken the most brutal pain a human can feel and turned it into something sacred. Something useful. Something that saves lives.

She didn't just return .. she resurrected. She turned her grief into a raging fire. Her silence into a roar. Her scar tissue into a sword that cuts through the lies we tell ourselves about what's possible after loss.

I've learned more from Melissa than I ever anticipated...about pain, purpose, resilience, and what it really means to rise. And I can tell you this: once you witness her story, once you let her words sink into your bones, you'll never see your own pain the same way again.

And that sword? It now cuts through the darkness for others.

This book is a miracle.

Not just because it's brilliantly written, or because it's packed with wisdom (which it is), but because it almost didn't exist. The woman who wrote these pages almost didn't come back. The pain she endured...the gut-wrenching loss of her baby girl Leyden ...nearly took her out for good. And it would've made sense if it did. No one would've blamed her.

Because there's no pain more unnatural, more soul-crushing, than losing a child.

But Melissa...She didn't run from the pain forever. She found her way to this place, but it wasn't easy. She had to finally meet it head-on. And she let it carve her into something rare, something beautiful, something untouchable.

Her story is littered with lessons. I've learned that the greatest people in the world often come from the darkest, most painful circumstances. She is, without question, one of the most powerful and gifted human beings I've ever known. And I don't say that lightly.

Her story...what she's lived through, what she's built from the ashes...isn't just inspirational. It's essential. Because the truth is, we're all going to grieve. That is quite possibly the biggest lesson that will change your outlook on life once you read this book. Grief actually looks like many different things. Grief is not just about death. Melissa taught me that. There are countless types of grief! Grief for what was, what could've been, what should've been. We grieve relationships. We grieve lost dreams. We grieve missed time, broken promises, invisible wounds. Some people are grieving and don't even realize it. They just feel numb, stuck, and disconnected. And that's why this book matters.

Because Melissa cracked the code.

She figured out how to take the most painful human emotion on earth... and turn it into power. Purpose. Fuel. Legacy. Not by bypassing the pain. Not by sugarcoating it. But by doing the hard, holy work of standing in the fire and finding the light within it.

And here's what I want you to know about Melissa: She doesn't just talk about this.

She LIVES it.

She's one of the most giving, servant-hearted leaders I've ever witnessed. She'll show up for you when no one else will. She'll hold space when your world is falling apart, and still find the strength to lift you out. I've watched her carry ten times the weight anyone should have to carry...and still ask, "How can I support you?" #FACTS !!!!!

She gives. She serves. She heals. She builds up others!

And this isn't because life's been easy for her. It's because she's earned her scar tissue.

She's paid the price in blood and tears and silence and nights that no one saw. As I'm sitting here writing these words, I'm reflecting back to how we wrestled with book titles, with truth, with how to name the unspeakable.

And "Scar Tissue" kept surfacing.

Because that's exactly what greatness is made of.

Not perfection.

Not having all the answers.

Not being untouched by pain.

But having the courage to let your pain shape you...NOT destroy you.

That's what Melissa is. She's a diamond.

A woman who was shattered, and somehow used those shards to carve a new path not just for herself, but for you. For all of us.

If you've ever hidden your grief... If you've ever worn the mask...If you've ever smiled on the outside while dying inside...This book is your permission to take it off. To come home to yourself. To feel it all and to well again. With power and purpose.

Reading this book will change you. It will call out the places in your heart that you've locked away. It forces you to look in the mirror. In the places you have hidden from the world. It will validate your pain. It will challenge your story.

And it will show you the truth: your grief is not your end. It is your beginning.

Because when grief gets pointed in the right direction, it becomes purpose. It becomes impact. It becomes the most sacred gift you'll ever give the world.

And Melissa Dlugolecki is proof of that!! Her words are sacred. Her presence is rare. Her mission is unstoppable. To witness her rise is to believe in resurrection. To read her story is to remember your own strength. And to apply what she teaches...is to be set free.

So read every word. Let it hurt. Let it heal. Let it awaken the parts of you that forgot you were still here for a reason! Because if she could come back from that...she would be the first to tell you that so can you!

This isn't just a book. It's your roadmap back to your own soul. And Melissa? She's the guide you didn't know you needed. Until now.

Melissa, thank you for the powerful perspective and the bright light you have gifted the world that was birthed out of the hell that nobody should ever have to experience. Leyden's beautiful life is now saving countless other people's lives. She has brought you the purpose that will guide you to the rarest places in life...A place of real significance and real impact. You are a world changer, and humanity needs to hear this message. It's an honor to stand side by side you as you rise to your greatest self.

Erik Rock

Foreword

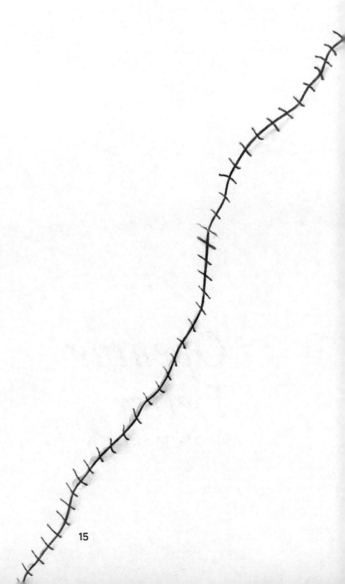

*Opening
Letter*
FROM MELISSA

"It's too heavy; I don't think I can share it." I remember exactly where I was standing as I spoke these words out loud, pacing my tiny office in the back of my apartment in Watertown, Massachusetts.

The knot in my stomach felt like a boulder. And I felt like I was going to vomit.

"That's exactly why you have to share it, Melissa," my former coach responded.

Sharing about grief and my journey felt impossible at first. I poured hours into crafting both the Facebook post and obituary announcement that shared the news around the death of my daughter, Leyden. The only post prior to it was a photo of her, healthy, just a few weeks prior. I asked friends and family to review and re-read the announcements so that it wasn't "too heavy."

But really, how could the death of my daughter, in a case termed "a catastrophe" after unexpectedly spending ninety-nine nights of her four-month life in the hospital, with a "routine case" turning into four surgeries, life support, and leaving the hospital without her, not feel heavy?

This book was not a sudden decision or declaration. It's been a slow evolution of processing the many lessons grief continued to teach, how it shaped me, and most importantly, how those applied widely beyond myself or my daughter's loss and supported hundreds and thousands of other individuals in their losses too.

From my observations of the discomfort collectively felt around discussing grief, the avoidance of this "taboo" subject only amplifies the power and devastation grief has on us.

Initially, I had a small group of people closest to me whom I emailed with some updates and what I called "Lessons from Leyden." Eventually, I nicknamed this group "Team Leyden," and together we shared experiences, fundraised for charity in Leyden's name, and explored the stories of not just Leyden but so many others impacted by grief.

But within these conversations, I discovered that grief was so much more than loss or death. And, it was a universal experience. Why is something that is arguably one of the very few things every single human on this planet will navigate seemingly swept under the rug of our world, as if talking about it or learning about it would it make worse? In my studies, it was the avoidance of talking about it that amplified the loneliness, confusion, and pain.

Grief weaves an intricate and unavoidable thread, touching us all at some point in our journey. It is an emotion that knows no boundaries, transcending culture, age, and circumstance. While grief is an ever-present companion, each individual's experience of it is as unique as our own DNA. There is no one-size-fits-all model to grief. In this book, we embark on a profound exploration of grief, understanding why its traditional stages and defined "types" aren't fully sufficient in the realities of the losses we endure. We will not only broaden the more traditional approach to the stages of grief but we widen the types of grief, the categories defined putting each person's grief into a little box. The reality is, your grief may fit into many boxes and go through many stages at the same time. It's not as linear, predictable, or categorizable as it has historically been approached. And that is okay. Understanding that is a key factor in experiencing relief knowing that there is no pressure for you to feel, or label, your experience a certain way.

While I will share pieces of my story, and there may be parts that are difficult to read, this is a compilation of global and individual case studies and examples to relate to your journey. Grief includes both collective grief we have experienced including the world shutting down, the mourning of our children in trafficking, or shootings as well as individual grief, which for you may present as the loss of identity, marriage, relationship, job, empty nest, pet loss, infertility, and more.

This book is designed to be a toolbox, a hug, and a thought expander.

I do want to lovingly communicate to you that there may be parts that are challenging to read or that evoke memories or reminders of your own losses. In fact, had I read this book in the earliest days of my grief, I wouldn't have been ready for it. I might have felt angry that someone could tell me I would grow through the worst loss of my life. But as you will read, it is in the courage to show up and only in truly allowing those feelings to come up and out that we release them. If we trust that, we can actually celebrate any tears as they are part of our healing.

We will not focus on the traditional five stages of grief. The five stages of grief, also known as the Kübler-Ross model, were introduced by psychiatrist Elisabeth Kübler-Ross in her book On Death and Dying, published in 1969. These stages represent the emotional responses that individuals may experience when faced with the prospect of their own mortality or when dealing with the loss of a loved one. It's essential to note that not everyone will go through all of these stages, and the order and intensity of the stages can vary from person to person. I encourage you to replace the misleading nature of stages that have a start and end date as experiences that will come and go and to remain open to there being more than these five, or even the updated seven, stages of grief that are so neatly organized on charts throughout many grief resources and books.

It's not that these stages don't exist, it's that they don't fully capture the timeline, lack of linear structure, and width of emotions that come with grief. Think of the journey as a curly straw. You know those straws that have two or three circles on them. As you progress through your grieving, you will inevitably go through loops. But every time you reach the low point of a loop, when you are continually doing the work, the bottom of the loop will be what was once the top of a previous loop. It takes patience and trust, but it is worth it, and it is possible.

Your grief will push into spaces beyond denial, anger, bargaining, depression, and acceptance. And it will experience many of these emotions, among others, in a cyclical way.

Furthermore, we will add to the currently defined seven types of grief, which again place confines and a box around an experience that can already feel suffocating.

These seven types, though defined slightly differently by different sources, most commonly include: bereavement grief, anticipatory grief, disenfranchised grief, ambiguous loss, collective grief, complicated grief, and cumulative grief.

Trying to fit our grief into a box or our emotions into a stage, in my experience, worsens and slows down our healing. It can add shame and comparison, two incredibly heavy energies, onto an already heavy experience.

While I was shaking at the first thought of sharing more widely outside the safety bubble of "Team Leyden," I learned and saw how the lessons I shared supported others in their lives—with their own parenting, their relationships, jobs, losses, and more. Slowly, I began to expand the lessons I learned as a student of grief. Those emails turned into a blog, then podcast episodes, and eventually many public speaking opportunities.

One of the larger venues I spoke at was Gillette Stadium, outside of Boston, Massachusetts. If you aren't familiar with this venue, it is home of the professional football team, the New England Patriots. On the drive to the stadium, where I would be speaking at a massive yoga event, raising money for Boston Children's Hospital, I was staring out the car window and noticed I was shaking.

It wasn't that telling my story was scary.

I lived it.

Telling it was easy.

It was the fear of it being "too much" for other people.

Too triggering, too sad, too heavy.

Even as I shared more, the first few times I shared about grief, I deleted my posts.

After hiring my podcast editor, I avoided answering his emails and completing the onboarding process for months.

And years later, as I wrote the final chapters of this book and publishing became a reality, the same fear I faced so long ago resurfaced.

What if it is too much?

The funny thing about grief, as I explore in this book, is that it doesn't really create anything new, it just pulls up the things that live inside of us and amplifies them massively.

For me, "too much" had been a story I had carried for a while.

I've never really fit inside a box, I don't live my life according to a checklist, and my tendency to go all-in on things resonated differently with people throughout my life.

So of course, my grief journey continues to teach me to break through that fear and to heal that part of me.

You will find that whatever grief you are experiencing will flush out things inside of you that you have been carrying long before this grief came into your world.

When we can quiet the chaos and whirlwind, we see that grief actually provides a space to heal at a level much deeper than the current loss experienced.

What allows me to choose getting uncomfortable and sharing things that aren't often talked about is my why: the belief that it not only honors my daughter, Leyden, but just as importantly, it serves others.

From one podcast episode, one blog post, one speech on grief...messages began flooding in.

People contacted me for support.

Emails sharing with me how what I shared changed their life.

Even as a pioneer and voice in the space of grief, on a mission to stand in the fire and talk about the things we often avoid talking about, I still get nervous, uncomfortable, and afraid it will be "too much".

When we avoid being in conversation around the less popular dinner conversation topics, we give them more power. My mission and goal is to empower you, to support you in seeing that you are stronger than any circumstance you have been through. That without toxic positivity or dismissing the pain of your grief, you can grow through it. To see how grief and growth can coexist. And that when our worlds feel shattered, we can employ the supports and resources to piece them back together, one by one.

Trust that in order to shift the narrative on grief, we have to begin to talk about it. To sit in uncomfortable spaces. To widen the definition of grief from loss of life to any type of loss that interrupts our feelings of safety and/or identity in the world.

So as you begin reading, I encourage you to bring a notebook and pen, as this is filled with action steps and prompts to focus your energy within your own journey. And most importantly, I encourage you to celebrate your courage, your willingness.

Thank you for being here. Thank you for your courage to look at the spaces that are not easy to look at. Thank you for believing in yourself and your possibility enough to invest time into your greatness. I believe in the masterpieces within all of us. And I believe in our ability to allow each scratch, cut, or wound to allow us to be even more beautiful versions of ourselves.

In love and gratitude,
Melissa

HOW TO
RESPOND
TO TOXIC
POSITIVITY

When we are grieving, it can be uncomfortable for people. In an effort to lighten the discomfort, often times people will say "positive" things. I understand this. In many cases, people don't have the skills to navigate pain. Try not to take things personally. But we can use our voice in how we respond. So after each chapter, I've included a common "toxic positivity" statement with examples of 3 types of responses along with a reframe:

1. **Non-Response** (people you won't see again/ or just not worth your time)
2. **Boundaried Response** (people you want to keep out and train how to talk to you)
3. **Educating Response** (people you want to let in and teach how to support you)
4. **Reframe** (not taking it personally, knowing they are uncomfortable in your pain)

These examples are written for people who are looking forward and healing while also allowing the reality of their emotions to come up. There are many nuances to everything, so please note the examples I share are not meant to be a blanket "one size fits all" response, but rather a tool you may find helpful in navigating grief and responding to toxic positivity.

PART ONE

THE WOUNDING

I remember the **moment** *the nurse walked in, and I* **knew** *before she said a word. My whole life* **shifted** *in that instant.* **Nothing** *would ever be the same. But* **neither** *would I.*

CHAPTER **1**

Drowning Out Grief:

ACKNOWLEDGING THAT THE WOUND BEGINS AND ENDS AS A BLESSING

There is a specific sound a breast pump makes. A mechanical and artificially rhythmic *wah-wah, wah-wah, wah-wah*. I never noticed how inhuman it was until the day after my daughter died.

With each pump the *wah-wah* taunted me, as I sat sprawled on the cold, empty nursery floor cruelly reminding me that while my daughter had passed, my body was still intuitively mothering. Biology lags behind emotion. I was no longer a mother, but my body acted like I still was. Tears poured down my face.

I had no idea who I was or what my life was going to look like. The future I envisioned had been ripped away. The deepest love I had ever experienced was now the deepest pain I could imagine. I felt so much shame, confusion, and doubt. As repetitive as the sound of the pump were my cries asking out loud, "What did I do wrong?" yelling to drown out the *wah-wah*, and truly, a desperate attempt to drown out the pain. With each pinch of the machine on my breast I felt a pinch of shame.

"I am so sorry, Leyden; I am so sorry." With each scream came pangs of failure, of powerlessness. I am Leyden's mother. My one job was to keep her safe. And I failed.

The tears streamed down my face more quickly as I replayed the moment that felt too horrific to be true in my head. After spending ninety-nine nights of my daughter's four-month life in the hospital, I was accustomed to hospital living. It was our normal.

The truth was, even though the medical team had told us she was going to die when we took her off of the ventilator, I was certain she would live—which is a common response when you are in a state of trauma: the denial of the reality you are desperate not to face.

What supported my denial was that two weeks prior, my daughter had come off of a machine called ECMO, which is essentially life support. They said she would not live. At the time, our families and church came in to say their goodbyes. Everyone filed in and out, somberly. People brought food and hugs and were at a loss for words.

When it was time, the hospital staff shuffled my family, friends, and me into a private waiting room, a place where many families had waited before while a loved one took their final breaths. The room wasn't warm or inviting, it did not feel like a place you wanted to be while your child was being removed from life support. But it was there we waited, waited for the doctors to return with a solemn nod, indicating that she was gone.

After hours of tears and replaying video after video of Leyden for anyone who hadn't met the "healthy" version of her, the doctors came out to announce that Leyden lived. It was as if I had been snapped out of the depths of despair and flung into the bliss of hope, love, and trust—trust that everything was going to work out.

My feet took off before it had even fully sunk in, my daughter was going to live. My mind was racing, my heart pounding as I found myself in a light jog back to her hospital room. She had to live, she wanted to live, she needed to live. I ran to her side and looked down on her beautiful, little face. She looked tired, but peaceful. There she was breathing, all on her own. At that moment, my mind ignored what anyone else said, because my daughter was a miracle and she was NOT going to die. All I could think was, *this girl is going to live, no matter what.*

After Leyden survived the impossible, the doctors told me she would need to go on dialysis. It was another machine, another procedure that my baby was going to have to go through. But because she had lived, it felt different this time. It felt like this time the doctors were doing something not to make her more comfortable or give her more time with me, but because she had a chance that she fought for, on her own.

Her body began healing and the swelling went down. The green fluid that had been present disappeared. The redness in her eyes reduced. But underneath the external healing, her organs were failing. This promise and the hope of a life together was quickly fleeting. Despite having a fully functioning heart, a strong spirit and a healthy brain, my daughter's body was failing. NEC, renal failure, and organ failure were stealing her from me.

Weeks later, Leyden took her last breath. Her eyes were looking right into mine. Her body was swollen, tired, and limp. She was sweaty and cold at the same time. Her jaundiced skin was the shade of a burnt orange. I stared at her, crying, telling her that I loved her, praying that just like the last time, she was going to defy the odds and live.

When she took her final gasp of air, I stared at her, waiting for her to open her eyes and breathe again. *Come on, Leyden*, I thought. As the medical team removed my daughter's lifeless body from my arms, I immediately fell to the ground screaming.

I wanted a redo. I made the wrong choice; I fucked it up. I wanted to go back in time and fix what had been done. Without even knowing what was pouring out of my mouth, I began screaming in desperation, "I want my baby back! Nooooo! I want my baby back!"

Her father cleaned her body, preparing her for autopsy, and I laid in the fetal position, shaking, watching my nightmare become reality. The room was spinning. I was in complete shock. *This cannot be real*, I thought. When he encouraged me to crawl into her crib and hold her one final time, I hesitated.

Of all the freaking things to be worried about, I was somehow self-conscious of what the medical professionals would think. I looked around at the nurses and had a moment of *This is going to look so weird*. I stared at my daughter's dead body lying in her crib.

At that moment, I realized that nothing about my life going forward was going to be normal.

Why the f*ck do I care what anyone else thinks?

Nothing is okay, and nothing will be okay, so why am I so damn afraid someone will be uncomfortable?

My daughter is dead; I am uncomfortable.

I made the decision to stop caring about anyone thinking that I was "too much" or "weird." That moment was one of many in which my six-pound daughter would forever change my life. I crawled into the crib. I held her cold body against mine. I kissed her forehead, her cheeks, rubbed the thin bits of hair that remained on her swollen head. And then it was time to leave.

Before I could think, the words came spilling out with the tears. "I am so sorry Leyden. I—I am so sorry. This should have never happened. I am sorry. Please forgive me." The apology slipped out from between my teeth, as my body was shaking. I continued to apologize to her, hoping that her spirit was there, listening, knowing I did everything in my power to save her. That I loved her, even though I couldn't save her.

As I walked out of the hospital, with Leyden's things in hand, I dragged my feet into the car. I gently secured her stuff in the passenger seat, books, onesies, stuffed animals; all neatly piled and buckled in next to me. As I adjusted my rearview mirror, I stared at the empty car seat in the reflection. A cruel reminder that I wasn't leaving the hospital for the last time the way I had always envisioned. In a car full of "things," the most important thing, was missing. I realized that nothing felt safe or secure. Life as I knew it was gone. My future, taken from me.

I decided that I would never actually move on. How could I? Which is when I later realized that moving forward and moving on are drastically different, and too commonly entangled, concepts.

Being in the Discomfort

The truth is that so many people will tell you, "It will get better when..." because of their own discomfort with your pain. They will tell you that there are five stages and rush you through them as if every person experiences the spectrum of emotions in the same way. They will tell you that after a year, it gets easier. I am not going to tell you that.

But what I will tell you is that your grief is real. It's not exclusive to death. Grief exists in the micro and macro. It transpires daily. Whether it's the loss of a relationship, a job, a career path, or even changes in holiday traditions when the world is constricted—grief is there.

People hide from it—the discomfort, the awkwardness. But that only compounds our loss. When we don't know how to talk about something, we don't talk about it. And when that happens, we are only adding more loneliness, shame, and loss to our struggle. We create false truths to avoid the reality of the truth we don't want to see.

Strengthening the Scar Tissue

Grab a journal or open your notes app on your phone or use your laptop—writing is a key part of healing and I include many exercises in this book so having something handy will help. As you begin, set an intention for the pains you have experienced or are currently enduring and connect with them as you move through this book.

The Wound Begins and Ends as a Blessing

At some point, grief can shift from something incredibly painful and hard, into something transformative.

The pain will never go away. But I truly believe grief can be transformed. It can be painful AND beautiful. It can shift the POWER of pain into purpose...and I love this perspective so much.

I wasn't done being a mother. I wasn't done being Leyden's mother.

The pain doesn't stop, even when it is barely noticeable. I cried and shook in bed for what I believe was an hour. The pump finally stopped—a final *wah-wah*, and the battery died. No fading out. No getting weaker. It just stopped. My grief didn't.

My grief was all around me. It was beyond the battery powered pump. It was the books I had bought for her, each week of my pregnancy, with a hand-written note in it. The outfits my family spoiled her with. It was the stuffed animal my best friend had so lovingly picked up in a boutique while on vacation in excited anticipation for Leyden's arrival. It was her owl binky "Olivia" that we called her "best friend." The wooden letters that we had painted in the hospital, spelling out "Dream Big Little One" to hang on her wall. The custom print we ordered during a "shopping spree" from her bedside, with lyrics from a song reading "All the World is a Place for you to Shine." It was the grey rocking chair that took me months to pick out. I had fussed over if it was big enough or comfy enough for me to power nap on when I would rock Leyden back to sleep during those 3am feedings. Grief was the sage green color of her walls, the color that reminded me of my baby girl. I couldn't shut her door and keep grief trapped in there, although I tried. Grief quickly found its way beyond those four walls and into every corner of my life. My grief was everywhere.

That is the thing people don't get about grief. There aren't linear stages that you go through. You don't complete one and then start the next. Grief doesn't fade and disappear. You don't get over it. The battery running grief never dies. I thought, like the breast pump battery, that one day I would be over grieving, that it would end.

GLIMMER OF GOLD

Grief becomes a part of you, you do not stop grieving, you learn how to work with it and let it unlock your greatness.

You will never get through grieving. It will become a part of you. In this book, you will learn how to manage and integrate your grief. I am going to show you how to allow grief, as difficult as it is, to do its job. I will not show you how to stop grieving, because that makes it worse. I will not show you how to speed it up. What I am going to teach you, and those around you, is how to manage it.

The truth is, grief carries on. *Wah-wah*. But it will not control you. It will not own you. Grief, after all, is a device. And, as shocking as this may sound, it is designed to serve you. Grief can unlock your greatness. People often rush to push away grief, seeing it as a way of holding onto pain and loss. But grief isn't about the loss—it's about the love we hold. That's why we feel it so deeply. Grief reminds us of the love that still lives on, even after someone or something is gone. And that love, when embraced, has the power to heal us, not hold us back.

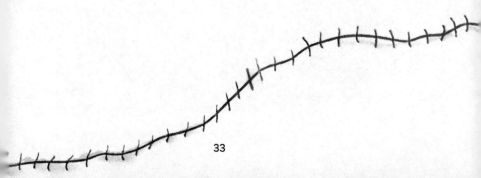

33

TOXIC POSITIVITY STATEMENT

"At least…"

Release: *Comparison to others or what could be worse.*

Responses:

Non-Response: Smile and re-direct or end conversation (smiling is optional)

Boundaried Response: "That doesn't really make a differ-ence in the pain I am feeling, but I understand that you are trying to make me feel better."

Educating Response: "That doesn't really make a difference in the pain I am feeling, but I understand that you are trying to make me feel better. What would be really helpful is for you to just listen in this moment and let me be broken, even if that is hard for you. Can you do that?"

Reframe: Yes that could have been true/worse, but that doesn't impact my experience or the reality of it. They are independent circumstances.

CHAPTER **2**

Authentically Grieving:

GIVING REGRET AND SHAME A PLACE TO LIVE AND BREATHE

"I can't sleep!" I wailed from the bedroom out to the living room.

Leyden's father walked in, looked at me, and said, "Do you think it might help if you had less of her things in bed with you?"

Confused, I looked around. Less of her things? I scanned the bed. Tangled in the covers with me were Leyden's blanket, four of her stuffed animals, a book, two of her hats, her snuggly jacket, and of course an eight-by-eleven photo of her face, placed right by my pillow.

The look in my eyes matched the tone in my voice as I responded a firm, "No," before turning back to my pillow and tears.

Understandably, in the moment, that was not a pleasant experience. But looking back, I can see that it was my own authenticity shining through in my grief. This concept is widely ignored in traditional counseling and coaching.

Too many experts create cookie-cutter processes, steps, "right" or "wrong" ways to go through the process. And this can actually add layers of shame when these so-called "good" ways to handle the deep pain you are experiencing do not work. Suddenly, not only are you feeling the extreme pain of your heartache, but you are feeling like there is something wrong with you for not grieving the way experts say you should.

Grief is Your Own

In my experience, nothing in life is a one-size-fits-all model, especially not your grief. The widely known five stages (now evolved to seven stages) of grief are well-intentioned and certainly supportive to identify different experiences that come with grief, but they can be counterproductive when creating a false illusion of control, as if we will go through one stage and then another and then another. Not only does this add pressure or rob a person of fully understanding their authentic emotional responses, the five, or seven, stages are missing many of the emotional experiences and phases of grief. I believe that these are all parts of, essentially, voices of our pain. Each voice will speak more loudly on different days. Some days anger will have the microphone; other days shock will reclaim it. Unlike sequential stages, the experiences of grief are not linear. They do not take the microphone, use their time, and hand it off to disappear. There will be days when they are all fighting for the microphone, days where one is very loud and others are quiet. And when triggered, voices that had been quiet may suddenly start shouting. The stages are also missing some of the emotional experiences that can be part of the grief process, which we will explore in future chapters. Alleviating the pressure of a timeline, a stage, or a category of grief (which we will also explore in more detail) is essential to healing.

GLIMMER OF GOLD
Alleviate the shame and guilt, give yourself permission to (responsibly) grieve in the ways authentic to you…

Space for the Healing

Nancy, one of my clients, felt like she should be "over it" by now. After decades past both her miscarriage and stillbirth, she was embarrassed by her lingering grief and pain. When we started working together, it took her months to share her losses with me, out of shame for feeling like she "should" have moved on already. Without ever having had the tools to deal with her losses and trauma, she coped by filling the emptiness by overeating, binge drinking, and relying on others to fill her up and make her feel happy. It wasn't until we began from the start again and completely abandoned the ways she was forced by societal norms to feel pressured to heal, not talk about it, and move on that she was able to finally stop decades of self-destructive patterns that were impeding her happiness and health. It was removing the feeling of something being wrong with her and her feelings that created the space for the healing to begin.

Grief (and life) need to be authentic.

Part of why Nancy struggled to heal her grief for decades was because she didn't feel like her loss fit in any actual grief category. The widely adopted seven types of grief have some slightly different iterations but most commonly include:

- **Bereavement grief:** Grief after the death of a loved one.
- **Anticipatory grief:** Grieving that occurs before an expected loss, such as when someone is terminally ill.
- **Disenfranchised grief:** A loss that's not openly acknowledged, socially mourned, or publicly supported.
- **Ambiguous grief:** A loss that lacks closure, for example a missing person or the loss of a connection with someone who is still physically present.
- **Collective grief:** Shared grief experienced by a group of people.
- **Complicated grief:** Prolonged, intense grief that lasts more than twelve months.
- **Cumulative grief:** Multiple losses over time, which can amplify the grieving process.

Permission to Grieve

While Nancy's grief could be considered to "fit" in the category of disenfranchised grief, because it's not talked about, she didn't give herself permission to grieve and as a result never healed. This is very common because by definition if someone's grief doesn't fit into a traditional box, they are not even clear on whether or not their experience is grief. I am here to tell you that grief cannot fit into any boxes. As a bereaved mother, arguably at the "top" of any grief hierarchy (I do not believe in any grief hierarchy), any loss of what was in existence or what you envisioned for the future carries the elements of grief.

I will never forget the relief one of my best friends shared when I told her that her infertility journey was one of grief or when a friend, who lost much of his adolescence and feelings of safety, identified that the years of sexual abuse he endured brought a massive grief experience with it. In order to heal, we must allow ourselves to be clear that what we are carrying is in fact grief. And grief is much more pervasive than the traditionally accepted definition of a loss of life. Just like our grief is uniquely ours, our healing needs to be authentic to our losses, our personalities, and our emotional needs too.

When Leyden was alive, I quickly earned the nickname "Mama-razzi" from the thousands of photos I took during her lifetime. I loved being her mom by reading her book after book, singing songs, choosing outfits. When she was sick, I hung pictures of her everywhere so doctors knew who they were treating, and her team could feel connected to her spirit, because her physical body was unrecognizable.

I spent many days in the hospital's children's craft room. I could put my hands to good use there, making Leyden a mobile to hang above her hospital crib. In the CICU, children couldn't have mobiles over their beds as it was considered dangerous—Leyden loved her mobile—so I made her a CICU approved, safe one. I recorded myself reading every book in her nursery, so she would always have a story to listen to during the procedures I couldn't be present for. I even filled clear baby bottles with marker ink and water each day to signify how much fluid was removed from Leyden. That sat next to a hand-written sign that said "Win The Day Leyden! Get That Fluid Off!" I wanted the nurses to know that Leyden's mom was paying attention.

It all happened in a flash. One day we were told we were leaving, going home after what felt like decades. I diligently packed her bags, put together a newly cleaned dress and baby booties I had recently picked out for this exact occasion. I imagined all of the coffee dates with friends awaiting us, how we would chat in between sips of almond milk lattes and Leyden's smiles as she played with a teething toy in the stroller next to me. My friends and me peering under the brim of the stroller to see a happy, healthy baby. This was about to be my reality, it was going to be Leyden's reality.

But then the next day, the doctors told me something was wrong. And before I had time to even ask a question, there Leyden was, tubes going into her neck, nose, and stomach. Everything hooked up back to *that* dreaded life support machine.

A machine that was run by a staff member 24-7 that kept her alive. Her abdomen was open, and her intestines exposed. Blood oozed out of her belly. Her skin was completely discolored, the shade of burnt leather. Her entire body was puffy, as if someone had inflated air into her limbs, face, and chest. She almost looked like a Cabbage Patch doll that was overstuffed. When Leyden would open her eyes, they were yellowed and bloodshot. Her hair was falling out, and fluid had gathered at the back of her head so it was pear shaped with extra swelling at the base of her neck. I couldn't feed her or hold her, and there were minimal spots I could touch her. I feared that the people making round after round would see a dying body and become desensitized to the life trapped inside the decay.

Me? I saw her spirit. I saw her eyes opening at the sound of my voice. I saw her wiggling her toes and fingers when I touched her and pressed my face to hers. I saw her manage to raise her right arm overhead, her signature move, regardless of the doses of morphine received. I would have to whisper to the doctors during each procedure, because no matter how much morphine they gave my baby she could hear me and would flutter her eyes or wiggle her toes and fingers. All because she heard the sound of my voice. I would go home and collapse into my bed, I felt powerless in all of it. There was nothing I could do. But the next day I would get up, put on a face, and be Leyden's biggest advocate.

I knew for doctors and nurses, I needed to make sure they saw beyond Leyden's physical state and made sure the pictures of my healthy, smiling, and loving baby girl were staring at every single one of her caretakers.

It was only natural that after Leyden died, I would enlist the same strategies and tools of sharing "love" as I did when she was alive. Beyond the artifacts I kept close to me when I attempted to sleep, I had a number of Leyden's things still in my car too.

Her car seat in the back offered me a closeness whenever I looked in my rearview mirror.

Her bathing suits on the floor of the backseat were a reminder of our plans.

The imprint of her hand sat in my cup holder, an acknowledgement of our reality.

I needed to cling to all of them for a while: to feel Leyden with me, to sing to her in the backseat, and to hold her hand in the front seat. To ask her to lead the way. To bawl my eyes out and to shout in anger, in pain, and in confusion. I needed all of it. It was my authentic experience. I was authentically grieving.

Honoring Your Process

Textbooks might question the wisdom of my having Leyden's things in my car and sleeping with them.

Me? I say it was authentic.

And I'll go even further.

It was an important part of my own process.

Intuitively, I was clinging to what is termed "linking objects" in grief.

Linking objects are the things that "link" you to the loss. Without knowing that linking objects are an actual "thing," so many of us naturally align ourselves with the places, smells, foods, things, and sounds that help us feel closer to the loss.

You probably find comfort in linking objects without realizing it. Maybe it's a sweatshirt of your ex's that you miss, a photo of someone who passed, a necklace that was handed down to you, or going to a beach, restaurant, or destination that you shared with a person at one time in your life. From closeness to this place or object, you feel more closely linked to what you are missing.

Had I been denied the opportunities to fully express and communicate love and mothering in the depths of Leyden's loss, I would have had gaps in my healing. Major gaps.

On the other hand, Leyden's dad did not find comfort in linking objects.

Having pictures, things, and especially clothing around didn't offer him comfort. While I wanted to talk about Leyden nonstop, he preferred to hold her privately.

Luckily, the words of my grief coach guided me to understand that "the biggest challenge relationships face isn't the loss itself but the expectations of the other person to grieve the same way." I was able to let go of claiming one way to be "right" or "wrong" and rather just allow each way to be. This was an important lesson for me to learn, not just in grief, but in life. Rather than dying on the hill I stood on, I chose to just let people be.

One of my one-on-one coaching clients came to be infuriated with the way her husband was managing the coinciding loss of his job and the divorce of her parents. It was as if she had prepared an opening statement for a jury to prove to me (her jury) exactly why her husband was handling things the "wrong" way in hopes I would affirm that she was doing it the "right" way. When I taught her the concept of authentically navigating these adversities, she was deflated and became quiet. It wasn't until about a month later that she shared with me that very conversation not only allowed her to better understand her parents' divorce, it contributed to her avoiding divorce. Had she not implemented these tactics I had given her, she would've created more distance between herself and her husband. She would've created more grief.

Strengthening the Scar Tissue

What brings you comfort during times of pain and grief? Do you find comfort in linking objects? Do you prefer space to distance yourself from your loss or trauma? Is it possible to recognize either path as serving this purpose, without judging yourself or shaming yourself for allowing yourself to authentically heal the emptiness?

Remember that your grief journey will be constantly evolving and unfolding. There will be times where linking objects feel more important than others. Rather than judging it to be right or wrong, allow your truth in any given moment to speak more loudly than judgment and create the space for it to fluctuate. There was a time when I posted on social media when my "L" necklace broke and had the store and friends running in circles to help find a replacement. There was also a time when I chose not to wear it anymore. Neither were right or wrong. They were both important parts of my healing. The more we remember that we are worthy of and likely going to change what we want and need, the more space that not only creates for ourselves but for the allowance of other people to authentically grieve their way too.

Growing Through Heartache

As we have talked about, grief is heavy.

The weight of shame, fear, or guilt around accessing, aligning, and filling our own needs is not an additional layer to be added. I encourage you to not only give yourself permission but to embrace your authentic ways of processing your grief. This may actually include choosing not to grieve at times. For example, Bereaved Mother's Day is a day I have spoken to communities of bereaved mothers and provided support, but it is not a day that I personally grieve. Perhaps if I had another child who was alive, I would want to have a separate day for both my living and passed children. But without that, I don't want to "miss" out on Mother's Day. It's already painful enough to not have Leyden on that day. To then also feel like I am "bumped" or "demoted" to an alternative holiday, for me, felt worse. For others it feels like an important acknowledgment. Remember, there is not a right or wrong in how we choose to align our energy.

Now, this doesn't mean that there isn't a level of responsibility with grieving authentically. I didn't have the right to go lash out at people, be hurtful or destructive, and disguise it as authentic. If I only laid in Leyden's things without any intention to move forward, I wouldn't be taking responsibility for my healing.

Sandy, a thirty-two-year-old lawyer whose eight-year marriage ended against her wishes, hated the concept of "personal responsibility" for our healing. And I didn't blame her. I hated it too. I remember feeling angry that on top of losing my daughter, I now had to take responsibility for navigating my excruciating pain responsibly. I was pissed. So when Sandy pushed back on this concept, I was ready with compassion and understanding but also with a commitment to helping her see that while she didn't welcome her divorce, and of course when she said her "I do's," she never imagined the hell she was now living from her world being divided in half, it was ultimately her choice to move forward productively.

After a few weeks of making space for the anger and feelings of betrayal (a very necessary part of the process), Sandy was still reluctant to let go of the "It shouldn't be this way" feeling. Knowing she was ready, I looked at her and offered, "Let's write out our options for moving forward." I continued to explain that sure, I could be a place for her to vent about her ex, and I was willing to do that. But I wasn't convinced that was best serving her needs and growth. So I asked her to break down her options and choose which one she wanted me to coach her toward. Going through this process, she was able to identify that she wanted to grow through her heartache and welcome in a new sense of normal and happiness. Her identification of this granted me the permission I needed to move her toward taking personal responsibility and actively pursuing the path to get to where she wanted to be.

Tools for Healing

Grieving authentically is a magical dance between allowing space for our emotional needs while taking action toward growth. Progress comes from striking a balance between the internal reality of the chaos and pain that comes with loss and the external reality that the world will continue on, the sun will rise again, and people will return to their normal lives. It's recognizing it's our job to identify and honor our pain and also our job to choose to move through it—and to enlist support and resources in aiding us to do so.

This breaks us free from the often pursued patterns of trying to "wait it out," as if things will get better after enough time, or of relying in a dependent way for a person, a job, foods, drinks, or entertainment to absorb and carry our pain for us.

There are three major concepts to understand when it comes to grieving authentically and taking personal responsibility for doing so.

1. We can't suddenly use a new tool.

When sh*t hits the fan, our life crumbles before us, and it feels impossible to breathe, we aren't suddenly going to use a new tool to "feel better." So thinking that all of a sudden you are going to take up meditation if you have never meditated isn't realistic. When the walls are falling in, and you are barely staying afloat, a new skill, source of comfort, or tool isn't going to work. The ones that will work are the ones you have used before. What tools are currently accessible for you? List them out.

2. Understanding ourselves is critical.

Well-intentioned people who want you to heal will start talking about all the ways in which you "should" heal.

"Won't her pictures make you sad?"

"It will get better when..."

"Are you sure you still want to talk about it?"

"At least it's not..."

"You should have another kid."

"Time to move forward."

"Get a puppy."

"When did THEY say you will get over it?"

Your emotions will pull at you, significantly. When others pull at those emotions and try to steer you in directions that align with THEIR comfort level, awareness of yourself and your needs will allow you to stay connected and authentic through the healing process.

3. Adding to your toolbox is an important part of authentically grieving.

Just because we don't have a tool when we start grieving, doesn't mean we can't cultivate it. This is a huge benefit of grief groups and grief coaching. Not only do you have a place to process, you will expand your toolbox. Perhaps trying meditation once a week, to slowly find it comforting rather than attempting to force it each day, works for you. Maybe it's beginning to read or write more intentionally. Maybe physical activity offers release, and that local batting cage you have never been to is suddenly calling your name. What are two to three new tools you can intentionally integrate to provide you with more outlets for the pain? These will not be your "defaults" immediately, but over time, they will expand the resources and support available to you.

Strengthening the Scar Tissue

Make a list of things that you find supportive. Reflect on things people may have done that felt supportive or things you feel may be supportive, that aligns with what is authentically you.

My client Amy's tools for handling the pain of her beloved dying were to overexercise, put on a strong front, and control everything she could possibly control in her life. She had been conditioned to stuff down her fear and stress because it made others uncomfortable. How did this play out? She was over-committing, scatterbrained, and missing meetings and appointments. At night she would numb her pain with an extra glass (or three) of wine and console her anticipatory grief with comfort foods she typically denied herself. The next day, she would feel shame for her choices, overexercise, and repeat the cycle of denying her emotions, putting on a mask, and continuing forward. In order for her to stop exhausting herself, this pattern had to be interrupted. The only way to interrupt the pattern was to practice using new tools, a little at a time, each day, until they became comfortable. Phone-a-friend, crying, boxing, and journaling became new tools she employed that not only provided places for her to process and confront her emotions, they replaced the patterns that added stress, guilt, and shame to an already intense situation.

I'll never forget when one of my college roommates brought massive posters that I had ordered for Leyden's memorial service to my house. I hadn't seen her since Leyden passed, and when she came in carrying a stack of posters of Leyden, she said to me, "All right, I am only giving these to you if you promise not to hang them on your ceiling and stare at them all day."

Beyond using her gift of humor, Lauren was calling out what was authentically me—emotion, sentimental and pouring out love. She had memories of me making scrapbook after scrapbook for four years of college.

She knew my defaults.

And while I didn't hang the posters on my ceiling, they certainly did come in handy.

Months after Leyden passed, I learned of a tradition at my church for "El Dia de los Muertos" (The Day of the Dead)—a time when my church community would honor and acknowledge all those who had passed.

When I heard this, I jumped with excitement. I was going to be able to say Leyden's name out loud! People would know her! She would not be forgotten! All these thoughts raced through my head as comfort rushed through me. My biggest fear was that Leyden would be forgotten. When I learned that I could bring a picture of Leyden to the altar, my heart leaped. People could see her face!

Then of course stress set in as I began overanalyzing which photo to bring.

I asked my Reverend which photo to bring, and she said, "Bring all of them."

So I did. Every single poster sat on the alter during that service.

And now I invite you to give yourself permission to bring all of what is most authentic for you to your grieving process as you build your world and look to creating your new life.

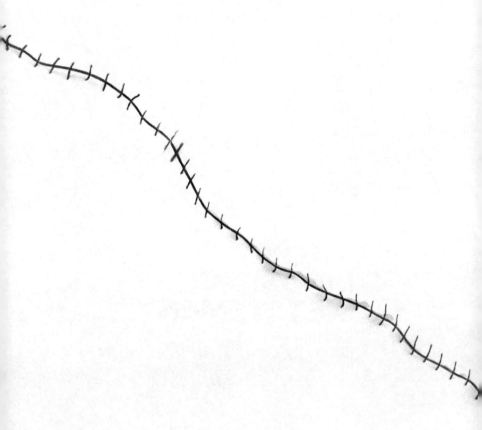

TOXIC POSITIVITY STATEMENT

"Everything happens for a reason…"

Release: *Self-blame for punishment or trying to "find" the reason.*

Responses:

Non-Response: Smile and re-direct or end conversation (smiling is optional)

Boundaried Response: I am not in a place to try to find a reason for this.

Educating Response: I am not in a place to try to find a reason for this. I know that is commonly said, but making sense of this just makes me feel like I did something to deserve it or has my mind racing anxiously to try to find the reason which only makes me feel worse right now.

Reframe: I don't need to know or find a reason. There may or may not be one. Right now I need to focus on healing one day at a time and trust that everything else will unfold over time. Other people seeking to assign meaning to this does not mean I need to.

CHAPTER **3**

Knowing Your Capacity:

A COURAGEOUS AWARENESS

"Hey," my friend answered the call.

It was a usual call. I was sitting in my car, seemingly the only place that felt confined enough to hold me, private enough, and safe enough for me to spend hours. Sometimes I would spend hours driving, not knowing where I was going. It was as if I could physically move when emotionally and mentally, I couldn't move at all.

Without saying a word, I started bawling. "I miss my baby! I want my baby back!" I wailed into the phone.

"I know, Melis. I know. Let it out."

At the time, I wasn't aware of the learned behavior, almost a survival mechanism I had developed to know whom I could call in those moments. For me, there were only two or three people who served to fill my team as a "listener."

Grief isn't the easiest subject matter. It's not a topic that is welcomed at dinner tables, social events, or on holidays. When facing the depths of grief, you will find quite often that people react with unease and discomfort. Grief has a way of unsettling others, almost as if the raw emotions, unfiltered vulnerability, and the powerlessness we can all feel around it hit a "danger button." Friends and family may offer well-intentioned words of solace but will struggle to find the right words or actions. In their discomfort, some might withdraw, fearing they lack the wisdom or strength to provide adequate support. Others may offer quick-fix solutions or attempt to distract you from the pain, unknowingly avoiding the profound reality of loss.

The truth is as a society, we aren't the best listeners. We want to fix, help, solve. We may feel uncomfortable with the discomfort of others and try to rush through it, make it better, or even pretend it doesn't exist.

Here are six hard truths I learned from grief:

Disclaimer: if I read these when I was new in my grief journey, I probably wouldn't have been ready to "hear" them. But these truths from grief changed my life. I hope these serve you.

1. We don't need to feel good all the time. And we don't need to feel "good" or "bad." We can feel pain and gratitude, love and loss, all simultaneously. Putting pressure to define our state with one way of being will not serve.

2. Gratitude and trust are the medicine. Someone asked me how I feel about my loss and I said, if I could use one word, it would be trusting. If I could use a second, it would be grateful. The power is in feeling these things unconditionally, not just when things go your way.

3. There is radical responsibility in grief. This is hard when grief naturally lends itself to a victim or pained energy. Choosing to be in responsibility for our experiences, our needs, how we communicate what is coming up, will catapult your growth in all areas of life.

4. Not everyone will get it, and that is OK. Let go of the expectation of people to show up in a certain way, respond a certain way or support a certain way. When we truly release expectations like this, it's freeing. Honor each person's capacity and comfort without making it right or wrong AND be sure to still take care of your needs.

5. The body keeps score. All these years later, I can feel the milestone dates in my body even if they aren't consciously in my mind. Do the work in your mind and your heart, but don't forget to work the body. Move, release, and let go of the emotions that find their way into our vessels.

6. Some people will avoid because they don't know what to say, some people will toxic positivity because they are uncomfortable with the heavy. Don't take any of it, or anything, personally. Giving your power to their reactions will drain you of your energy.

Working On Capacity is a Daily Practice

Grief doesn't just break your heart, it redefines your capacity.

Have you ever experienced a moment where you literally just didn't have the energy to answer a text, an email, a phone call? Maybe even from someone you normally are excited to speak with?

Or days where your body physically struggles to move?

I will never forget a time when I was so excited to go see a musician I loved perform. I finally felt ready. After a long period of not being able to listen to music, I could feel my capacity build. I could tolerate music, laughter, conversations more than when Leyden first died.

That's the thing about capacity because as it builds, we have to work with it daily to gauge where we are at. One day it might feel like a great idea to do something, another day, seemingly inexplicably, it feels like too much.

I walked into the show with my girlfriends. I felt my throat tighten. My body tense. My eyes began to water. Before I knew it I was whispering "Sorry, I can't, I have to leave." Before hurrying home in an uber to cry myself to sleep.

A night I had been SO excited for. Dressed up for. Thought I was ready for, but I wasn't. The crowd, the noise, the witnessing in such a loud way the world all moving about like nothing had happened (humbling aspect of grief because it's a reality).

Which was just feedback of new ways to start to understand and work with capacity.

One of the most important things to understand about navigating grief and loss is that your internal resources shrink. Things that were once easy may now feel insurmountable. Conversations that once felt light might now weigh heavily. The emotional, mental, and physical energy you once had for life, work, and relationships may no longer be accessible, at least not in the same way.

This isn't a personal failure. It's biology. It's humanity. It's grief.

In fact, 90% of grieving individuals report a reduction in their ability to concentrate. And while no data supports this opinion of mine, I believe 100% are impacted and the 10% who reported they are not, are not present to the impact they are experiencing.

I always joke that my dog, Tajin, the sweetest pug in the world, is my "capacity" monitor. For example, when I walk her each morning, she never changes. She likes to explore, is curious, and will sniff a leaf for an hour. Meaning, Tajin is the **constant** to hold a mirror to the **variable** of my capacity.

Some days I see Tajin poking around and take pictures or think "Aw, Tajin, you are so cute! Do you love that leaf?"

Other days I notice annoyance and I will think "Tajin, what is so interesting about that damn leaf, we need to keep moving!"

Tajin hasn't changed.

My capacity has.

Being Aware is a Flag for Support

Understanding capacity and the limitations of it as well as the fluctuations of it on a day-to-day basis is an instrumental part of navigating grief. When we have an awareness of our capacity, we can plan accordingly. One of the best ways to get clear on it is to allow ourselves to be the variable while comparing our reactions and emotions (which are ever changing) to a constant.

An easy example of this could be your morning commute. Let's say you leave the same time each day, drive the same route, and there are predictable bits of traffic. If you find yourself some mornings enjoying the drive, noticing the sunlight or a bird, your capacity is likely spacious. On the other hand, if you observe some days feeling impatient or flipping radio stations because nothing sounds good to you, your capacity is likely limited. The commute didn't change; your response to it did.

The reaction and response is the variable a great indicator of capacity (or emotional space/room) on a given day.

Take a moment to think of where you can witness your reactions to be the variable next to a constant or routine.

For my clients, I teach this concept through the visual of a tank.

At times we will draw on the tank what is "filling their space" to see how much room they have.

Some days, they have room to take on new things.

Other days, they are filled.

And at times, they are overflowing and need to prioritize removing things from their energetic environment.

Beyond it being feedback for you, it will also serve as a flag for when you need to call on support, BEFORE things completely fall apart. Waiting until we are overflowing before taking action is a quick way to find yourself in a cycle of burnout and exhaustion, breakdowns, and potentially creating more exhaustion from avoidable arguments that then drain even more energy.

We overflow because we let pain compound; with my clients I call it compounding pain. Similar to compounding interest. It builds overtime until it reaches a tipping point and overflows. We need to deal with that pain before it can reach that point of extreme overwhelm.

Capacity is your ability to carry, respond to, and move through the demands of life—emotionally, mentally, physically, and spiritually. It fluctuates constantly, especially during grief. It's not a measure of how strong you are, it's a reflection of what your internal system can manage in the *present moment*.

When you aren't aware of your capacity, you risk pushing past it and paying the price—burnout, miscommunication, emotional outbursts, or disconnection from yourself. Grief lowers capacity, so being aware allows you to move with more care, make wiser decisions, and avoid compounding pain.

It's really important to not compare our capacity as a "right or wrong" on a given day. Just allow it to be what it is. Adding judgment to our reality only intensifies the weight of what we are carrying.

Here are a few ways to check in with different aspects of capacity:

Mental: Am I thinking clearly or feeling foggy?

Emotional: Do I feel grounded or fragile?

Physical: Is my body energized or depleted?

Social: Do I want connection or solitude?

When we are building awareness, much like at the gym, we need to know when to push ourselves to **strengthen** our capacity and endurance, and we need to know when to pull back. This connection to self and level of discernment is one of many hidden opportunities of grief because when you commit to this you can build an unwavering level of self-trust and self-knowing.

When you notice shifts, it's time to check in to see if you should push through (gently), or if you need to pull back. Just like at the gym, you build the ability to carry more over time, but if you go too all-out, too-quickly, or ignore signs from your body, you risk injury or doing damage.

Some signs that your capacity is stretched:

- *Struggling with simple tasks or decisions*
- *A shorter fuse or emotional withdrawal*
- *Physical fatigue or tension*
- *Saying "yes" when everything inside says "no"*
- *Feeling disconnected from joy or purpose*

Honoring Your Capacity Without Judgment

The truth is honoring your capacity doesn't have to be a negative. Doing "more" isn't always the path to growth. And having really honest conversations with yourself and others around you, can forge connections.

- *Decline invitations without guilt AND with honest communication about your needs.*
- *Reschedule or delegate tasks at work—with gratitude for the support.*
- *Delay tough conversations until you're in a better space by explaining that the conversation is important to you and want to be in*

the right space for it.
- *Prioritize rest over productivity—and know that rest can be productive.*
- *Choose presence over performance which strengthens your ability to let go of what it looks like or the opinions of others (which is a growth super-power)*

Each of these choices is an act of self-respect. And the people who respect you, will respect your needs. You will also build your ability to not over-commit which will help in all aspects of your life. Shifting from over-committing to intentionally-committing can build trust with yourself and with the people in your life personally and professionally.

"Back to normal" is a myth. I believe that we learn to create a "new normal" but the pressure to return to "as things were" is literally impossible.

There is a subtle, often unconscious pressure to "return to normal" as quickly as possible after a loss (which is further explored in Chapter 4 and after every chapter throughout this book that examines "toxic positivity" statements and responses.

The truth is, grief does not run on a schedule. Healing takes time, and more importantly, it takes space. The old normal is gone, and a new normal is being shaped in real time. In that in-between, your capacity will fluctuate, and it's essential to learn how to honor that.

When we ignore the reduction in our capacity, we risk overcommitting, over-functioning, or emotionally shutting down. We say yes when we should say no. We push through when we should pause. We try to show up for others in the same way we did before. Even though we're not the same.

This can lead to breakdowns: physical illness, emotional outbursts, strained relationships, or deep exhaustion that feels impossible to shake...It only compounds the pain of our grief and isolation.

We do NOT want to compound our losses with more conflict, challenge, or pain. Which is why understanding capacity is a non-negotiable in healing.

What to Do When You Have No Capacity

When I teach capacity, I tell my clients to envision a tank of air. Imagine the ones that you use to fill balloons. A full tank has no room for more air, or it will explode. This is a little bit different than thinking about "full cup" meaning we are fulfilled and can take on more. Full, in the context of capacity actually means we have no space to take on *more*.

When there is room in the "tank" we can manage things more easily. When there is not, we are vulnerable to arguments, snapping, or having a breakdown.

Honoring your capacity means getting honest with yourself. It means asking, *What do I have to give today?* and adjusting your life accordingly. And if you have a dog like me, perhaps your morning walk with your pup is the perfect time to check in on this.

One of the most compassionate things you can do during a time of loss is communicate your limits clearly and proactively. This doesn't mean you need to share every detail of your grief. It simply means being honest about what you can and cannot handle.

For example:
- *"I'd love to be there, but I don't have the bandwidth right now."*
- *"I'm still healing, and I need to keep things simple this week. Thank you for understanding."*
- *"I really want to support you, but I don't have the emotional energy right now. Can we circle back in a few days?"*
- *"I can't take anything additional on right now, I genuinely wish I could, but I just do not have the emotional ability."*

The people who truly care will understand. And if they don't, that's useful information too. Everything is feedback in the process of grief (and life) for you to pay attention to, so you can craft your Team (explored in the chapter of Teammates) and your energy, accordingly.

GLIMMER OF GOLD
By communicating your capacity, you protect yourself from burnout, and you give others the gift of clarity. It's a courageous form of self-respect.

When we pretend we're okay when we're not, we pay a high price. We become resentful, reactive, and more prone to lashing out or withdrawing entirely. The pain of grief doesn't go away just because we ignore it; it simply moves deeper, showing up in unexpected and often harmful ways.

This is how we unintentionally hurt ourselves or others. Not because we're bad or broken, but because we're stretched beyond what our nervous systems and hearts can carry. I will never forget some of the hurtful things I said because I wasn't present to my own pain. And while I wish I could take them back, what I found was the only way to show my regret was to commit to learning.

There's an invitation in grief to move slower. To take on less. To feel more. To rest more deeply. To protect your energy like a precious resource.

Notice what you turn to to distract yourself from the pain; alcohol, substances, shopping, fitness, busying in work, relationships, etc. can all be ways in which we avoid doing the work or sitting with the pain.

When Leyden died, I sat in my therapist's office one afternoon and she said words that I will forever remember. She said, "Melissa, sometimes you just have to sit with the sh*t."

I didn't know exactly what that meant. A few days later I noticed anxiety and discomfort in my body from grief. My reaction was to text some friends to see if they wanted to go to our favorite local Mexican restaurant. I realized what I was doing and paused. Then I noticed I began creating a checklist of errands I needed to run. Once again I noticed what I was doing and paused.

Wanting to run, distract, and scream, I surrendered. I looked at my couch. The silence and stillness of my home. And I sat. Until I cried. And then I sat and cried some more. After my eyes dried up, there was nothing left to create any more tears. I felt as though I was a fly on the wall watching a shell of a human. Watching as she was slowly consumed by her couch. She was crumbling before my eyes, and I needed to help her. I realized right there, I was alone. That was the release that created space in my "tank." Running around doesn't create space in the tank. The only way to create space is to process and let something out.

Strengthening the Scar Tissue

Each morning (or evening), take five quiet minutes to ask yourself:
- What is my capacity today—emotionally, mentally, physically?
- What's one thing I can let go of or say no to in order to honor that?
- What's one supportive thing I can say or do for myself today?

Write down your answers, even if they're simple. Over time, this small practice helps rebuild the habit of self-trust. It teaches you to listen, adjust, and move through grief with gentleness instead of pressure.

Remember: your worth is not measured by how much you can carry. It's measured by how honestly and lovingly you care for yourself when the load is heavy.

You don't have to be everything to everyone. You don't have to keep up appearances. You don't have to prove your resilience by pushing through.

Remember, you can say no. You can change your mind. You can ask for help. These are not signs of weakness. They are signs of wisdom. They are acts of self-love. Grief taught me that self-love is not bubble baths or spa days. It's emotional intelligence, honoring our truth, setting boundaries, and meeting our needs. While it's a lot harder than going to the spa, it's more deeply loving (and free).

What can you give yourself permission to cancel to create space for yourself?

Sometimes we wake up with a heavy heart and the best choice we can make is responsibly communicating to others and rescheduling that big meeting for the day.

Ordering takeout instead of cooking, again.

Letting the laundry pile up because your soul needs quiet more than clean clothes.

Ignoring the text messages or phone calls until you are ready.

And one of the most important things in understanding capacity is putting our Teammates in place to support us, which is the focus of the next chapter.

The good news is that capacity, like the tides, returns.

Not all at once. Not in predictable patterns. But slowly, steadily, your heart will find more room. Your body will hold more energy. Your mind will begin to clear. You will feel the difference.

But it happens because you honored your limits, not in spite of them.

There is strength in that surrender. There is wisdom in that restraint. There is love in that letting go.

TOXIC POSITIVITY STATEMENT

"They say it gets better after a year..."

(insert whatever length of time they say)

"They say it gets better over time..."

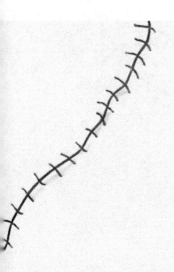

Release: *The pressure of a timeline.*

Non-Response: Smile and re-direct or end conversation (smiling is optional)

Boundaried Response: Respectfully, I don't want a fabricated timeline placed on my process.

Educating Response: Truthfully, I have heard all different timelines, and I think it is important to know that it is different for everyone. What would support me the most is just being with me in my own timeline; can you do that?

Reframe: No loss, challenge, or heartache is the same, and a timeline is an attempt to feel control over something that is not controllable. Release trying to control or other people trying to feel in control.

PART TWO

THE INTEGRATION

Grief didn't ruin my life. It *revealed it.*
The truth. The edges. The resilience I didn't
know I had. It made me *rebuild* with
intention. There is no "right" way to grieve. No
timeline. No clean ending. And anyone who
tells you otherwise hasn't *lived it.* It's not
about fixing or erasing the hard. Grief becomes
a part of the story you carry. But it never
gets to be *the whole* story.

CHAPTER **4**

Hope is Dangerous:

REPAIRING YOURSELF DEEPLY

It was Father's Day 2014, I left the hospital where my daughter Leyden was in the CICU, for just a couple of hours and was at my parents' house having dinner.

When my dad asked how Leyden was doing, I responded "Fine, the same." And then I paused, I felt it in my body, the knots, and I said in words that weren't even present to me, "Leyden cried for the first time today."

Just one tear rolled down her cheek. From my baby girl who'd been in the cardiac ICU for what felt like forever. Her body was unable to move as she was hooked up to so many wires and tubes. Her abdomen, open. Four surgeries (3 of them unanticipated), and this was the first time I had seen her cry in a month of being in the CICU.

She didn't even cry when she defied death when they took her off life support two weeks before.

The same little fighter who we'd promised, through prayers and tears, that we'd keep fighting this battle for as long as she led the way.

That single tear should have been nothing. But somehow, deep in my soul, I knew. She was trying to tell me something. Something I wasn't ready to hear.

A few days later, the doctors delivered the news: Leyden had 0% chance of living.

I fought it. Hard. I refused to speak to anyone except one attending Cardiologist, a mother of five who wasn't even on duty. She had left her family and her home, to come in and meet with me. When I heard she was coming in, I knew it wasn't good. She was a mother just like me, she would understand. I refused to have this meeting with anyone else, it had to be someone who could understand my maternal instinct to ensure my daughter's survival.

And with more love than I thought possible, she looked me in the eyes and said: "Melissa, the only dissenting opinion is that we could have had this conversation sooner, but we wanted it to work so badly for you guys and for Leyden. But now, Melissa, she's beginning to suffer."

That's when it hit me. That single tear was my baby girl showing me she was tired. She was leading me just like we'd promised. Not leading me where I wanted to go, leading me to let her go.

Sometimes the greatest act of love isn't holding on. It's letting go. Even when it shatters your heart into a million pieces.

Because true love—real, raw, earth-shattering love—sometimes means the allowance of what is no longer serving, working or healthy, over the pain of losing it.

When Leyden died, well-meaning people sent tons of messages to me to try to soothe the pain. I realized how many people, including at times myself, try to stuff down the pain or gloss over it with "Of the positivity". The reality is every single person has experienced grief. Or currently is. It is the most universal experience we all inevitably face.

So instead of making it weird, avoiding it or trying to muscle through it:

Can we learn from it?

Observe it?

Witness it?

Doing the Deep Work

Energy can't be created or destroyed, but it can be transformed. What we attach it to will significantly impact our happiness, levels of overwhelm, and stress levels.

Every single thing we take in will either add to our energy or deplete it. This holds true for thoughts, words, books, podcasts, TV, social circles, conversations, foods, drinks, and more.

One of my primary focuses for not only myself but for the people I support is an energy inventory. It's kind of like an accounting check to see if we are pouring more out than allowing in. I like to think of it as a bank account.

Are we bouncing checks?

Or making deposits?

It's slightly ironic how much I love this approach because I used to dodge my dad whenever he tried to teach me how to do balance sheets and budgeting.

But it works.

And in doing so, I discovered one of the sneakiest ways that people feel drained.

They believe that they are thinking positively or opting into environments that are happy, light, and constructive.

In reality, these spaces are destructive.

There is a difference between doing the work on ourselves to heal and gaslighting our own experiences or allowing them to be gaslit by others.

One of the fuelers of this is toxic positivity.

Toxic positivity is the excessive or insincere promotion of positive thinking and emotions at the cost of dismissing or invalidating the genuine difficulties and pain that are being experienced.

There is a difference between a growth mindset that focuses on how to strengthen ourselves through our experiences and a toxic positivity mindset that ultimately tries to hide or sweep our experiences under the rug and pretend they don't exist. Toxic positivity is often a factor for delayed grief or breakdowns years after a traumatic or painful loss occurred.

Toxic positivity will view emotions such as sadness, anger, or frustration as "bad."

I frequently invite you into different ways of thinking, but in this instance, I am urging you to look at where you label an emotional experience as right, wrong, good, or bad.

The stages of grief do a disservice, as we see them as something to "get through"—anger is a stage that we can go through and complete. The reality is, anger is a very human experience that will be amplified during different times in your grief journey.

If we make it wrong, we are adding shame to it. If we think it will conclude, when it inevitably pops up again, we will try to stuff it down or avoid allowing this very real experience to come to us, move through us, and be healthily released.

Here are some key characteristics of toxic positivity:

- *Denial of negative emotions*
- *Minimization of struggles*
- *Invalidation of feelings*
- *Pressure to stay positive*
- *Lack of empathy*

The slogan "Good Vibes Only" is plastered on coffee mugs, tee shirts, hats, and stickers that adorn much of our world. While well-intentioned to remind us that we have the power to think positively, it creates a pressure and judgment around less comfortable experiences. It implies that we should not feel, experience, or express anything that is negative.

I don't actually believe that anyone intentionally chooses toxic positivity. Sometimes, it is an automatic response from societal programming. Other times, it is a subconscious decision to avoid feeling uncomfortable. Our nervous system will almost always choose a familiar hell over an unfamiliar heaven. In the closing chapters, we will explore both how subconscious programming leads decision-making and how to break free of autopilot, as well as the ways our nervous system is impacted through grief and tools to regulate it to get out of the fight-or-flight state that will often lead to defaulting to survival rather than growth mechanisms.

While well-intentioned, statements that rely on hope, waiting for it to get better, getting "over it," or just "think positive" may dismiss the person's pain and emotions, making them feel guilty or invalidated for experiencing grief. In fact, if I could rewrite the quote the seventeen-year-old version of me said to her class at high school graduation, "Don't cry because it's over; smile because it happened," I would have her say, "Go ahead and cry because it's over. Cry it out. Let it out. Let your tears flow. And make time and space to smile and laugh for all that you experienced. Cry and smile, whenever you want. Do both."

Some of the common phrases that are associated with toxic positivity include:

"Stay positive; everything happens for a reason."
"You should be grateful for the time you had together."
"Don't cry; they wouldn't want to see you sad."
"Time heals all wounds; you'll be fine soon."
"Think positive and you'll attract positive energy."
"Sadness is a sign of weakness; be strong."
"Focus on the good memories."

These statements minimize the depth of the person's loss, imposing a pressure to feel thankful rather than allowing them to process their grief naturally. They encourage someone to stop themselves from releasing the emotion and instead stuff it down, and can create guilt for a person grieving to feel a certain way, or shame and confusion around the very real emotions that arise.

Avoidance is Not the Answer

I had the BEST system for managing my credit card bills and financial health when I was in my early twenties. Credit card bills would arrive at the same time each month. And I did the same thing every single time: ignored them.

Fearful of what I would see when I opened them, or looking at my bank account and knowing that I needed to wait another week or so to pay my card, I just thought if I let it sit there, it might magically sort itself out, and a solution would appear.

Maybe I would get a raise, an extra shift, or somehow find myself in the presence of more cash flow.

Too unsure of where to start or how to manage it, I simply "hoped" it would resolve itself somehow.

As you can imagine, this "system" that I embraced left me $100,000 in debt—with terrible credit and a heightened overwhelm with finances so that I wanted to ignore them more.

Eventually, I got myself into a situation where I had no choice but to deal with it. And I had a whole lot of interest accrued on those initial balances. My dad still likes to remind me that the glass of house wine I bought in Italy when I called from a pay phone to raise my credit limit cost me about the equivalent of the nicest bottle of Barolo wine you can find.

Similarly, we accrue interest on our grief, trauma, and heartaches when we hope it will magically get better.

There is a balance between what I consider to be a growth mindset that focuses on growing and positive outcomes and leveraging hope as a form of avoidance.

Having learned my lessons from my credit card companies, I knew that "hoping" my grief would go away was not going to serve me well.

However, the misbelief that "It will get better when..." can really lure in that human side of ourselves that doesn't want to go to the places we need to go to in order to heal.

Nina came to me for support. It had been over twenty years since she lost her infant child and shortly after had a miscarriage. Her large family offered support but would say things like, "Let's talk about things that are more positive," or, "Don't you think it's time to move on?" While they were concerned about seemingly stagnant sadness (unmoved grief), they were not equipped to understand the depth of support that she needed.

She filled her social media feed with inspirational quotes, spoiled her nieces and nephews with gifts, and developed a codependence on her living child all in attempts to bury her pain. But, like whack-a-mole teaches us, when we stuff it down, it just comes back up.

For Nina, this manifested through binge-eating, drinking to numb, over busying herself, and avoiding being alone as well as avoiding being in silence. If there was a quiet moment in our session, she would quickly look to fill it. When we first began working together, she didn't think that her unhealed grief was at the root of so many of her challenges. She simply wanted to lose weight and improve her marriage and her relationship with her daughter.

What we uncovered were the patterns and dynamics that she had created as a survival and coping mechanism and that grew over time. They were "accruing interest" in the direction away from her healing, compounding the initial "price" of grief, and adding a whole lot more to it.

GLIMMER OF GOLD

We cannot wait for things to get better to feel better, we need to feel better to create a reality where things get better.

Cultivating a Growth Mindset

An alternative to avoidance and toxic positivity is a growth mindset. A growth mindset can include feeling anger, sadness, rage, pain, loss. A growth mindset doesn't mean we do not feel these things; it's a mindset that allows us to mold these emotions in a direction of growth rather than stunting it.

Each moment we form habits, muscle memory, and emotional patterns.

When looking to cultivate a growth mindset, think of it like a muscle that you train.

Just like we can train our bodies with consistency and intention, we can train our brains.

And much like how each of our fitness plans or programs would differ based on our unique state, our emotional fitness training needs to be individual to each of us.

Similarly to our physical health, the longer we spend our emotional health moving in a direction away from where we want to be, the more we have to "undo" to get to where we want to be.

For Nina, not only did we begin working to grieve the losses she endured, but we worked to grieve the losses she felt for the way she had been operating in her fight-or-flight nervous system response for the last couple of decades.

One of the practices I used with Nina and have supported over a thousand other individuals in implementing, is a daily manifestation practice. Manifestation, mantras, and affirmations are all supportive tools in retraining your brain to focus energy on areas that support your growth. However, many of them are missing the component of action. Words without action will remain thoughts and words. The practice that I teach not only draws on the law of attraction, it simplifies daily action steps that can be taken to generate momentum. Just like we can accrue interest when we ignore the credit card bills that add up over time, we can also accrue credit in the direction we want to move that will add up over time too. The trick is to not put so much pressure on massive growth happening overnight but rather to get just a little bit better each day.

If you aren't familiar with the law of attraction, it is the philosophy or belief that like attracts like. It works with less tangible and scientifically based concepts and ultimately states that what we focus our energy on will grow. The law of attraction is rooted in the belief that where energy goes, energy grows. In the practice that I work with, there is both thought and action combined around intention setting and leveraging the law of attraction. You can access my entire free training and worksheet on www.scartissuebook. com, and this six-minute daily practice truly has the power to change your life through working on generating awareness and choosing intentional thoughts and actions each day.

For now, think of the last time you bought a new car or perhaps a new set of luggage, pair of sneakers, or planned a trip somewhere new. Whatever it is, choose something that you spent a lot of time researching and looking into and then eventually purchased. Very commonly, people will notice after making a purchase that suddenly "so many other people" have the same color or model car, the same type of luggage, sneakers, or are vacationing in the same place. The reality is that not everyone else suddenly copied your purchase. It is that your energy and attention are more focused on the investment you made, and when your energy is focused on something, you tend to notice it more in the world around you.

This can apply to your healing in a way that works without toxic positivity.

The Be-Do-Have Model

Many times we focus our energy on what we do not want or what is missing.

I can't tell you how many clients I have worked with who can spend hours telling me what they do not like or want in their relationship or in their job. But when I ask them to share what they DO want, they are often at a loss for words.

The be-do-have model was one that was introduced to me six years after I started this manifestation practice. I was in an emotional intelligence training program, and a model that was taught demonstrates that it starts with our energy, then moves to action, and from there we have the result. Intrigued that this so closely mirrored the manifestation practice I had learned, I researched it further and saw that while it is widely used, there isn't a clear derivation. Napoleon Hill was an influential author and self-help pioneer best known for his book *Think and Grow Rich*, first published in 1937. In the book, Hill discusses the idea that one must first develop the right mindset (being) and take specific actions (doing) to achieve desired results. This ties in closely with how we authentically grieve. To develop the right headspace, we must first allow ourselves the space to do what feels authentic to our grief. We must be willing to authentically grieve before we can manifest the things we want out of life. It's only from a place of allowance and alignment that we create the room to receive. Without authenticity, we become energetically misaligned, creating blocks that prevent us from inviting in anything new.

The manifestation practice I coach is one that I started when I was $100,000 in debt, had recently invested over $6,000 in a coach, was very raw and new in my grief journey, and going through career changes. I didn't know how I was going to change my life radically, but I knew I needed to. I actually asked the woman teaching it to me if I could do one for different areas of my life: one for finances, relationships, health, career, and more. She laughed, said she had never been asked that, and encouraged me to get clear on the one thing that was most important for me to place my energy.

This highlighted something very important in grief: patience. In a society where we can instantly download things, access information more quickly than ever, and generate results in short timelines, healing takes time—but not in a way where time is what heals it. Time gives the space for the healing to happen, but we must choose into our healing. And it is a blend of both our thoughts and energy and our action.

The full manifestation training on my website, which I highly encourage you to access and practice, will go much deeper in how to align your words and actions daily. Before that, take some time to begin focusing on what you do want. Many times we seek to achieve a feeling from something that we have, but this practice will show you have to first start with the energy and feeling, the source and root of all that we create, to then have what we desire.

My daughter, Leyden, is still gone. If I waited for it to get better or for my unhappiness with her being gone to go away, I would still be waiting. On some days, all I could focus on was taking a shower and reaching out to a friend. On other days, I was able to write, go for a run, or put my energy to deeper forms of healing.

Strengthening the Scar Tissue

In order to grow through our grief, we must be intentional about how we are using our energy and training our minds to move out of autopilot, out of nervous system responses, and into a growth mindset. We can train our minds through visualization, meditation, and affirmations. Identify techniques that align with you and how you can be intentional with your energy.

A daily mantra to support in building momentum in the direction of healing is: "Today I choose into healing in the very best way I can, in each moment."

Mantras and affirmations can be a powerful way to support yourself in your healing journey. Here are some additional examples:

I produce, create, and elevate in the stillness, flow, and ease.

I am abundantly loved, guided, and supported.

I trust everything is unfolding as it needs to, even if I do not understand how or why.

I learn the lessons that present each moment and day.

I choose growth. I allow the discomfort of growth. I trust the process of growth.

I am open to exploring the unknown and reverence of possibility.

It's all available to me; I choose into my growth each day.

I am open to the opportunities the Universe presents.

I am the ultimate owner for everything in my life.

Love and support flows to me with ease.

No one needs access to me unless I allow it.

Maybe it is a mantra, an affirmation, or trying the manifestation practice. Choose one way that you can today, right now, begin to train your brain to allow your healing to be a process of strengthening your emotional agility.

At first you may feel uncomfortable repeating these mantras. You may not believe them, and they may make you angry or upset. The first time I spoke these, I burst into tears as the words left my mouth. I felt like a fraud. A failure. Let yourself flow through those feelings and continue on, repeating them daily. Eventually, you realize that what once felt fake is not only your truth, but your reality.

And while I write these tools and techniques, it's not lost on me that a growth mindset can be confusing in our hearts. We're saying affirmations and taking responsibility, and learning to appreciate our lives again. I could never be grateful for the loss of my daughter. But I could be grateful for what that loss taught me. That's the difference. Growth and gratitude does not mean approving of the pain—it means recognizing the power that can rise from it.

TOXIC
POSITIVITY
STATEMENT

*"_____ wouldn't want
you to be sad…"*

Release: *Guilt for your feelings and truth.*

Responses:

Non-Response: Smile and re-direct or end conversation (smiling is optional)

Boundaried Response: I think that _____ would want me to honor my feelings and truth.

Educating Response: When you tell me that, I feel guilty for experiencing sadness and that only worsens the pain. I know you are trying to help and thank you, but the truth is we don't know what _____ would want. And I like to think _____ would support me in expressing and releasing my feelings for my own healing and growth.

Reframe: I am worthy of expressing my feelings and it is healthy to move through them and release them, even if uncomfortable for me and others. I let go of projecting any assumption of how _____ would want me to feel and trust that they would love me through my messiness of human expression.

CHAPTER 5

Grief Cells:

ALLOWING GRIEF TO
BECOME A PART OF YOU

"They say it gets better after a year, right? Oh Melis, just hang on, it's almost a year."

What the hell are you talking about? I thought.

Coming from love, the woman speaking was worried about me, uncomfortable with my grief and seeking to make me feel better. So she pulled out the biggest misconception in the grief handbook: the one-year finish line. This idea and notion is that after a year we cross a magical finish line, get a trophy, and things are suddenly better.

Bullshit, I thought.

Unless someone is handing me Leyden when I cross that one-year finish line, this hell I am in is not getting better. In fact, I was dreading the one-year marker because it actually felt like pressure to have to heal. I felt like these voices were whispering at me to hurry up, figure this out. I imagined a timer with sand rushing through it, and when it ran out, so would my support. People would go from patient and understanding to looking at me wondering when I was going to "get over it."

The invisible clock only deepened my anger—there it was taunting me. Every second of the day I could hear it tick, as the one-year marker crept closer. But the clock wouldn't stop ticking after one year. It would only get louder, as if it were laughing in my face; a constant reminder that in place of where Leyden should be, grief was there instead.

In a way, looking back I wasn't sure I even wanted to heal, because in my mind that meant letting go of Leyden. I feared healing meant more loss. I've learned since then that healing would never separate me from her but rather bring us even closer together.

This fear added weight to my grief, and the unspoken pressure I was feeling made my world feel even more suffocating, which, as you know, having a harder time breathing in an already hard to breathe place is not ideal. When I call bullshit on the finish line of grief, people will often counter with, "Well it does get easier, doesn't it?"

And in a way, yes it does.

But that's not because our loss has lessened. It comes from three components:

1. *We have built a toolbox of ways to navigate it.*
2. *We have built trust in our ability to get through the days we don't think we will survive.*
3. *We have expanded our world.*

Expanding Our World

This concept of expanding our world is one that significantly supported me in my healing process and continues to do so today with every change in my personal and professional life.

There are two things that make this approach powerful. First, it does not reduce the size of our loss or heartache. If someone told me that in order to heal, I was going to have to reduce the amount of "space" Leyden consumed, I would still be in my most shattered state. Because if Leyden could be the "biggest" in my most shattered state, well, then that is where I was.

If you have felt fear or guilt around healing, as if doing so would betray, diminish, or undervalue the loss in your life, I see you.

And I am here to tell you that you can heal and move forward without reducing the amount of room the person or loss consumes. For me that was a nonnegotiable. I was not about to embark on a healing journey if the cost of that was reducing the space Leyden got in my life. (Of course, if you want your challenge or trauma to shrink or disappear, you can choose that too.)

GLIMMER OF GOLD
The loss doesn't get smaller; our world gets bigger.

The second part of the concept that I really love is that it feels liberating. We just covered how suffocating grief can feel and additional restrictions can feel unbearable. Well friends, this is just the opposite. This concept is spacious, empowering, and one that will challenge you to think of what's possible. It will encourage you to consider where else you can expand, what might be calling to you, or maybe to finally make time for learning that new language, taking up knitting, or completing that puzzle that's remained unfinished for years.

Building On to Our World

In the concept of "Expanding Your World," which you can see on this visual, the loss, heartache, and trauma don't lessen. They remain the same size. What changes is that you expand the places in which you devote time, attention, love, and energy.

So the healing is in reducing the percentage of space that your loss, heartache, or trauma consumes.

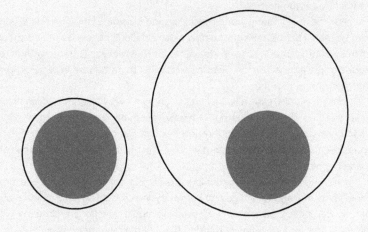

We don't wait for it to go away.

We choose to broaden our world.

Of course, the pace at which you do so will correlate with where you are in your journey. You are in the driver's seat. When I first started integrating this concept, I didn't want to build my world—Leyden was my world, so building it felt like I was losing her even more.

So how do we build? We start in places that are safe, and we start simple.

For my client Jessica, it began by working with me. After years of silence, I was the only place she opened up about her sexual abuse. Without realizing it, she was building her world by allowing someone else to stand with her.

Over time, as she felt safe, we began building her world in other ways and being strategic as to what level of intimacy each added layer brought. For example, sharing her abuse with her family, the police, and a couple of friends was a way of building her world, because for her, she was alone in knowing her truth.

On the other hand, it was also important for her to expand her world with new hobbies, relationships, and places to exist—and recognize that these didn't need to be spots where she shared all aspects of herself. These could be places where she simply received and experienced joy, excitement, connection and had fun. Fun was something she hadn't allowed herself to have after losing trust in the world as she knew it. So to build her world further, she joined a gym, a health club, a dance group, and even traveled on a retreat with an entire new community of women.

For me, building my world meant getting outside of my apartment, away from Leyden's things, talking with new people. I didn't have a lot of energy, and I didn't want to talk about much else other than Leyden, so I started with parent groups and with the Boston Children's Hospital marathon team twice a week. That was enough for me.

In both places, I still felt like I was seen as "Leyden's Mom," which helped make this first step of expansion. I highly recommend that you are thoughtful and get support in thinking through the first places you want to build your world, because they are instrumental to the trust you will build around the safety and happiness of doing so.

I had considered other running groups but realized that no one there would know me, and they wouldn't know Leyden. I would have to either explain that my daughter died when they asked inevitable questions around my work and my family, or I would have to deny that I had a daughter. I wasn't ready to explain my loss to people who wouldn't understand or have to worry about their reaction, and I was certainly not going to deny having a daughter. By slowly getting out of my comfort zone, it began to feel safe and possible to do so in other ways.

Here are some ideas for looking at ways to build your world. (Remember to keep it simple!)

- *Cooking classes*
- *Book club*
- *Running groups*
- *Joining a gym*
- *Art class*
- *Spiritual or religious groups*
- *Travel*
- *Learning a new language*
- *Podcasting*
- *Hiking*
- *Volunteer opportunities*

What might you add to your life?

The possibilities are endless, especially in this world that we live in.

One of my clients, Tara, a thirty-seven-year-old high school teacher, expanded her world after her fiancé cheated on her. She learned a new language and started selling health and beauty products on the side. From those two choices, she was suddenly exposed to new ways of speaking and witnessing many other ways people made a living. Before I knew it, she quit her nine-to-five and began traveling the world. She wrote to me from a Café in Europe to share that her integration of concepts expanding her world was something she chose to do every single day—and as a result, she had found countless new hobbies and made friends in various countries.

It doesn't always have to be extreme. Another client of mine, Deb, decided to use a friendship app on her phone twice a month where she created some new friendships while exploring different foods, wines, hiking trails, and movies through the various meetups the online platform hosted for in-person experiences. For her, these connections were local, intimate, and accessible enough that they didn't feel overwhelming but offered plenty of comfort and enjoyment back into her life after the painful loss of her father.

As you expand, you may notice that you need "recovery days." I like to think of these as emotional recovery days, much like how in our physical fitness we have to integrate days of physical rest in order to continue to strengthen and improve our fitness.

It's common to feel what Brené Brown terms as a "vulnerability hangover," or just simply exhaustion, when we begin to build our world. That's because as we do so, we are exerting energy, and our defenses are up extra high to identify potential "danger."

Just like training for a marathon (which I was doing, by the way), grief is a marathon. We cannot start by running twenty-six miles. We need to start with one mile and have the patience and perseverance to build our endurance, stamina, and strength.

As you build your world, avoid the common zero-to-one hundred trap where we want to do "all the things" to build our world and escape the pain. The truth is that it isn't actually building your world. That's avoiding your suffering.

Strengthening the Scar Tissue

Building your world is an intentional concept. It requires thought, action, and reflection. These also happen to be the three energies of the ancient Ayurvedic medicine practice: vata (thought), pitta (action), and kapha (reflection). To make progress in any aspect of your life, this system of beliefs states that we must cycle through these three energies to maintain balance. For example, to build your world, you must think about ways to do so (vata). Next, you take action on these thoughts (pitta). And finally, you reflect on how it felt and aligned with your goals (kapha). From there, you return to the thought stage and, with previous actions and reflections, prepare new and progressive thoughts on how to continue to move forward.

When you reflect on something that went well, focus on why it went well.

When you reflect on something that didn't go well, focus on why it didn't go well.

For me, what went well at first was that I was able to go to places where I felt like Leyden's mom and also didn't have to explain what I was going through.

Of course, having support and a non-emotional perspective in assessing these is really helpful. I recommend a counselor or coach, but if those aren't accessible, this would be a perfect time to lean on your "listener" Teammates, which we will explore more throughout the book.

Boundaries Create Safe Spaces

As we build our world, we also need to embrace boundaries. For most of my clients, when they begin working with me, they associate boundaries with being cold, apathetic, and selfish. The truth is, it's this very association our society creates with boundaries that leads to exhaustion, burnout, and unhealthy relationships. How do I know this so well? Prior to losing Leyden, I thought people who had boundaries didn't care. After losing Leyden, I realized that boundaries not only created safe places for ourselves and others, they were in fact a loving and considerate framework to integrate into our relationships.

When we build our worlds, not everyone needs to know everything. And, when people do learn of our difficult truths, it's not our responsibility to ensure their comfort. Boundaries allow us to use our energy to maintain responsibility for ourselves and provide others with the clear expectation and information they need to make the choices they need to make for themselves. It removes guesswork and alleviates the tendency to read into things or make assumptions. We protect our energy by putting up boundaries in places that drain us and by protecting ourselves from depths or intimacies for which we aren't yet ready. By being aware of our needs and capacities and placing boundaries accordingly, we protect ourselves and create reliable and steady environments for others.

In time, I slowly expanded to the worship committee of my church, the yoga studio, graduate school, and eventually, the local run group I initially feared. I spent hours preparing for the question, "Do you have any children?" I was so worried about other people thinking I was contagious and avoiding me or that they would feel sad and not know what to say. I was also very consumed with fear of denying that I had any children and, in truth, was confused on if I was lying if I said I did—because Leyden was gone.

I rehearsed with my grief coach over and over.

So when I was asked that question at the Marathon Sports run club social, I was able to look at the person and say, "My daughter Leyden would be [age]. Thank you for asking; I love the chance to say her name."

TOXIC POSITIVITY STATEMENT

"It could have been worse..."

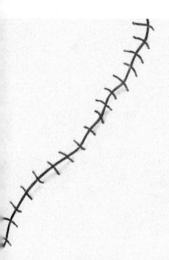

Release: Stifling feelings because something more painful could have happened.

Responses:

Non-Response: Smile and re-direct or end conversation (smiling is optional)

Boundaried Response: That's not really helpful, but thank you.

Educating Response: I understand that people go through things like this and much worse than this, but it doesn't take away the reality that I am navigating right now. I would love your support in just allowing me to be in my experience, even if uncomfortable.

Reframe: Every experience is independent; my reality has nothing to do with anyone else's and theirs has nothing to do with mine. I choose to honor my journey and allow others to do the same with their journeys.

CHAPTER 6

Forming Your Trauma Team:

YOU DON'T NEED TO PLAY COACH, CAPTAIN, AND PLAYER

"You wouldn't know; you aren't a mother."

Her condescending words pierced me like a dagger, plunged into my skin, penetrated my being, my heart, my world. She left me shocked, stunned, throbbing.

The mother of a high school athlete was in my office. She didn't have an appointment, and her emotions were clearly firing as she shared the injustices she felt her teenager was enduring from lack of playing time or being on the level team that she felt she was a fit for.

As I listened to her yell about the coach, I felt my blood pressure rising, my throat closing, my eyes swelling with tears, thinking, *I would give anything to help my daughter grow through the challenges of high school athletics.*

But when she looked at me and said, "You wouldn't know; you aren't a mother," it was too much for me to not respond. I knew my job was to listen, to be a bit of a customer service department. High school athletics demands a bit of politics and a lot of parent management when you are the head of a department. I knew the game I was supposed to play. But I didn't want to play it. I couldn't. I couldn't just pretend Leyden didn't exist, let the woman's assumptions about my life rule the conversation, and I certainly couldn't keep the bubbling emotion inside while simply nodding in sympathy for her.

While the pain was firing inside, I fought the urge to let it drive my response.

Instead, I sought to educate. "Lessons from Leyden" was an email campaign I had started after she passed when fundraising for Boston Children's Hospital. And living and sharing her lessons had become something so ingrained in me. I needed to let Leyden positively impact others. I had to represent her with grace. In this moment, it took all of my strength to bring grace.

Firm grace, I decided.

I counted. I responded.

"Actually, I am a mother. My daughter Leyden passed away four months ago. I understand your desire to protect your daughter from any pain. I watched my daughter live in excruciating pain for the last month of her life. I watched her fight and defy odds until her last breath. A breath that I still hear every time I close my eyes, sit in silence, and picture her confused gaze, locked squarely on me. A breath that she took with determination, only reminding us how badly she wanted to live."

She stepped back, looking shocked.

I considered apologizing for the directness of my message, already imagining the email that would be sent to my boss complaining about my response.

But at that moment, politics meant nothing to me.

Really, my job didn't either.

I just didn't care.

All I cared about was allowing Leyden's light to shine to make a positive impact. To teach others.

I continued, acknowledging her pain.

"There is nothing worse than standing by, helplessly and desperately trying to take away their pain yet knowing all you can do is try to counter it with love and strength. So yes, I know the suffocating feeling of witnessing your daughter encounter adversity.

"You are upset right now because your daughter is hurting. Your pain entitles you to ask for help. Your pain entitles you to get support. But it doesn't entitle you to tell me that I am not a mother and therefore cannot relate."

At a loss for words, she said she would be in touch and quickly left my office.

While I was shaking, hurt, pained, I knew that she was defaulting to a very common tool humans use when we are in pain: taking that fire of pain and throwing it at others—relief found through injury of others.

I call this the "hot potato" method. Yes, just like the game. Your pain is in your hands, burning them (badly), so what do you do? You throw it at someone or something else. You might feel better for a moment, but I promise you won't in the long run—because all you're doing is passing that pain along temporarily. What that woman needed in my office that day was support, not a game of hot potato.

I also knew that I was going to need support through this.

Assembling Your Team

How do we navigate the very humanness of our learned behaviors alongside the very realness of our emotional needs?

We learn how to assemble our Grief Team.

When we are grieving, there are two critically important things to remember:

1. *We have to allow our emotions to come up and be experienced to eventually be released.*
2. *Not everyone in our life can help us with each portion of that.*

Grief is ruthless, isolating, unpredictable, and incredibly lonely. One of the most challenging factors compounding it is that a lack of understanding or tools around grief can create wedges in relationships, which only worsens our pain. On the other hand, sometimes it can create codependency or what is often referred to as "trauma bonds." Neither of these options provides the landscape for grief to be a catalyst for growth. They deny both the griever and the supporter the space and opportunity to strengthen.

I truly believe with both the awareness and tools, grief can forge a pathway for deeper connections in a means that is healthy, boundaried, and mutually supportive rather than sourced in either distance or codependency.

This starts with taking full responsibility and ownership of our healing. Now, taking ownership doesn't mean that you need to do it alone. But as always, before we look outside, we start by looking within.

Grief humbled me. It reminded me that not everyone is waking up thinking, *I wonder how I can help Melissa, today?*

So it was up to me to get the support I needed in any aspect of my life.

The concept of assembling my own Grief Team was one that angered me in wondering, "Why am I now responsible for this?" and intrigued me to better understand the people in my life.

Think of your Grief Team much like any successful team that works together to create something one single person couldn't do alone. Perhaps you were an athlete. Not every person on a baseball team can be a pitcher. The pitcher requires a certain level of skill; the first baseman, a different skill. They need to have massive range to field the greater percentage of catches they need to make. The center fielder needs to have incredible speed and the ability to throw a long distance. The short stop is typically the most agile, able to cover ground, reach quickly, and throw the ball across the field.

This applies outside of athletics. Any band is compiled of people with different skill sets and contributions, same with theatrical performances, and the list goes on.

As a former athletic director, sports have been a huge part of my upbringing. Tom Brady is arguably (and forever in my opinion) the greatest quarterback in the history of the National Football League. He has statistically earned more records and impressive achievements than any other player to date.

However, throughout his entire career, there was one thing he was consistently teased for by sports announcers on social media and in the stands at games: he wasn't a good runner.

When plays were called where he, the quarterback, was required to run the ball, fans would hold their breath, and the media would often take clips of it that were used on highlights after showing how his running skills weren't, well, incredible.

Understanding Your Teammate's Unique Skills

I remember in early days of my grief journey spending hours running on the treadmill, particularly on the snowy days that filled so much of Boston's winters, training for the Boston Marathon I would run in memory of Leyden, watching Super Bowl after Super Bowl of Tom Brady and the New England Patriots competing. There was something about their unwillingness to quit that comforted me. I watched any behind-the-scenes interview I could—seeking stories of hope, resilience, perseverance, and grit.

And one morning while running, it was as if lightning came down and struck me with the understanding of my Grief Team.

If Tom Brady had been assigned to be a running back, he wouldn't have had the career he had, he wouldn't be the record-breaking success he was, and fans wouldn't be idolizing him and singing his praises the way that they do.

Putting him in a position to win—the position that matched his skill set—was the difference between world-changing success and failure.

So of course, I realized asking my brothers, who were less comfortable with the "heavy" stuff, to hold the heavy stuff wasn't setting them up to win or setting me up to get what I needed. But they could share their love in their ability to spend time, go to dinners, make me laugh, and other ways.

They had a unique and powerful way of saying, "I love you, Melissa," in a language authentic to them. Had I asked them to speak, "I love you, Melissa," in a different language, I would have created distance rather than closeness. I would have been unhappy thinking they weren't saying, "I love you, Melissa," when the truth was, they were shouting it loudly, in the way they knew how to. Just as it is important for us to grieve authentically, it is important for us to set up our Teammates in a way where they are authentically supporting. We cannot use a new tool in times of triggers. We also cannot expect others to speak a language of grief they are not normally fluent in.

I'll never forget visiting one of my brothers months after Leyden passed and the reprieve I felt from being out of Boston, distracting myself meeting his friends, exploring new places, and spending hours chatting over charcuterie boards and football games. It was a loud "I love you."

Nor will I forget when another one of my brothers came to visit me days after Leyden passed, and his knack for bringing levity to any moment shined through. As I sat in the living room, curled in a ball, he opened the refrigerator to boxes of leftover Chinese food, which happens to be his favorite. This guy could eat Chinese food every day of the week. He picked up an egg roll and turned to me, his face in shock. "Melissa, what the heck? This thing is like a dumbbell. I can't eat this!" When I told him I had eaten the other one the night before, his belly laughter was exactly the medicine my soul needed at that moment. My brothers also were my biggest fans along the Boston Marathon route, loved taking me out to dinner, seeing me have fun, helped feed the homeless on Leyden's birthday (bringing plenty of laughter throughout the day), and would allow me to cry on their shoulders whenever I needed to.

GLIMMER OF GOLD
People want to support but they don't always know how, and they all can support differently. No one can meet all of our needs. But everyone can meet a need.

I look back and see that by understanding their "grief languages," rather than asking them to speak their support in a way that wasn't authentic to them, we actually created closeness, connection, and memories.

There were times like I shared earlier in this chapter that I needed someone to just listen to me go on rants of rage, anger, sadness, pain, triggers. And other times I needed help doing things, moving energy by being active, doing projects in memory of Leyden, or simply just helping doing life things I struggled to find the energy to do.

The 4 Types of Teammates We Need
When I wanted to turn Leyden's outfits into a quilt, I asked for support from someone who offered help. I was comforted by the quilt, it was something

that was taken off my "to-do" list, and the person who had it made felt really good about supporting me.

The thing is, people WANT to support. It's just that often in grief, they don't know how.

Remember, no one is a mind reader. And no one excels in every area of support. But if you position people to win, you win too. And if you communicate clearly what you want and need and give them the space to opt in or out, you develop safety, trust, and connection.

No one can meet *all* of our needs. But everyone can meet a need.

That distinction is so minute and yet massively transformative in how we navigate the twists and turns of life.

So, how are we broadening this to look more fully at how we are assembling our own Grief Team?

There are four types of Teammates in grief.

- **DISTRACTORS:** The ones who best support you by taking your mind off of your grief. This is different than dismissing it—they acknowledge it, honor it, and respect it. When grieving, we need to take breaks from the heavy. It's like a workout—we can only manage intense periods for so long before we need rest. Distractors are there for the emotional rest. Their contributions will be doing activities or having discussions on other topics.

- **LISTENERS:** Most people think they are a listener, but the truth is, being a listener requires the ability to shelve their own emotional experience to hold yours. This means not saying things like "at least" or "it will get better when" or "when i went through..." They truly just listen to the deepest parts of your pain and ask how you want to be supported. Because of the difficulty of doing this for people we care about, it is often important to have a trained counselor or coach to support this role.

- **DOERS:** People who like to do all the things! For me, I enlisted an entire support team to help plan the memorial service, give feedback on my podcast, and plan charity fundraising events in memory of Leyden. Maybe for you these are people who love running errands, cooking meals, managing bills, tasks, or anything that can be taken off your logistical plate to free up more of your energy to go to your healing.

- **X-ERS:** No, that's not a typo. X-ers are a type of Teammate. At first you think, "Why would I want that person on my Team?" but the truth is, there are a lot of x-ers in the world from societal programming and human desires to be needed, be involved, or be in the know. X-ers are the ones who have patterns of inserting themselves into the drama or catastrophe of the week and let everyone know the updates. So, how do you leverage this type of Teammate to be supportive? Share anything that you want in wider circles. Think of them as your PR agency. All in all, X-ers can be a helpful ally in some situations. You may need to work with them at times, get the message across and control the state of your world. At other times, you will need to set hard boundaries with these people and walk away when you need to. X-ers can be an asset to your team, as long as you are aware of the possible consequences that may follow them.

TEAMMATES

DISTRACTERS	*Movies, Dinners, Comedy, Workouts, Drinks, Sporting Events, Concerts*
LISTENERS	*Sit in silence, hold it together while you fall apart, as how/if they can advise*
DOERS	*Grocery Shopping, Cooking, Planning, Events, Chores, To-Do's*
X-ERS	*The messages you want in the outer world, keeping you up to date (if wanted)*

Perhaps your Team has other types of Teammates on it. The important thing is to bring awareness and acceptance to the fact that not everyone can meet every need of yours, but each person can meet SOME need. Consider yourself the coach, director, or facilitator of the people around you and allow each of them to show up in ways that support you and align with their unique personalities and skill sets.

People want to help. They feel good when they do. When we ask them to help in ways that they can, rather than ways that they cannot, we not only receive more support, they feel much better and more empowered too.

I will note that this concept can apply far beyond grief. After studying it in grief, I began applying it to all aspects of my life—and it truly strengthened the connections between me and others in my world.

Strengthening the Scar Tissue

Write out a list of the ten people closest to you in your life. Identify which type of Teammate they are. Some people may hold multiple roles, and that is okay. But become clear on who is BEST in each area and ask them to support you in a way that works for their role. Finally, identify if there are gaps in your Team and needs. Fill them accordingly.

Once you have your Teammates in place, it becomes easier to navigate anticipated challenges such as holidays, anniversaries, and more. Innately, these milestone days bring memories of traditions or what it "should" look like. And it is likely that for you, there are layers of loss that feel extra heavy. For me, the anticipation of Leyden's birthday, Halloween, the anniversary of her passing, and other family traditions made it hard to breathe. I could feel it harder to find my breath, my anxiety at a higher level and overwhelming sadness and pain rushing through my body.

What I discovered was that when you feel like you are in a pressure cooker, finding places to take pressure off is not only supportive but required.

When we don't, suddenly we find ourselves crying in the bathroom at a holiday party or snapping at someone for something that normally wouldn't bother us.

I like to think of it as game planning. I remember as a field hockey coach spending hours drawing up game plans. Looking at the opponent's skill set, watching film, deciding which players on my team would match up best where, what corner plays would provide us the most advantage. And as always, since you cannot predict the weather, injuries, terrain, or the general unfolding of any athletic matchup, I had multiple plans in place for each event.

When applying this to grief, think of it as if you are putting together options to choose from on a day when making a decision or committing may feel like a breaking point. The truth is, when we are overwhelmed with pain, sadness, anger, hurt, any of the experiences of grief, making decisions or committing to something on top of that can push us over the edge. So what drives the pressure to commit to a plan?

For me, I found that many times it was self-induced, that I had to do the "right" thing, or know what was going to "feel best." But there was no way of knowing. Notice if you put any internal pressure on yourself when difficult days are approaching to navigate that in a certain way and see if you can alleviate that with compassion, spaciousness, and remembering that there will never be a perfect way to handle any of your grief. We do the best we can each moment, each day. Grief can invite you into that level of self acceptance—one that you can apply to your entire life.

A second place I witnessed pressure deriving was from people who loved me, wanting to know I would be okay on said day. Whether it was Leyden's birthday, Christmas, the anniversary of her passing, I was so blessed with so many amazing people reaching out to see what I wanted to do or how they could support me. The flipside of this was that I felt pressure to not disappoint them or cancel and felt anxious when I would make plans, wondering if I would feel up to it.

Recognizing that there was an opportunity to create connections while also giving myself the space I needed, I came up with a system of generating multiple "game plans." Leading up to the holiday, I would draft out plan A, B, C, and D. For example, "I would love to spend Leyden's birthday feeding the homeless and then going out to lunch, but if that feels like too much, would you be open to just spending time in the house? Or if I need to get away, would you be up for heading somewhere for the day? And if I wake up just unable to be around anyone, would it be okay if that morning I let you know I just want to be alone?"

I set plan "A" as the ideal plan and plan "D" as the "we are shutting it all down, I need to be with myself" option.

This provided the space I needed to be with my true emotions and experiences, allowed me to let my Teammates know that I am okay, and gave them the choice for how they can or cannot commit to what I was drafting for options. Part of my need to not fully commit also came with the need to understand not many people can just be on "standby," and that is okay.

I really don't believe that grief gets easier with time. To me, that's like saying a marathon gets easier. It's no shorter when you run your second, third, or fourth. The difference is that you are more prepared for it. You know you have survived it before, so the heaviness of the unknown is alleviated. The confidence in "I can do this" grows.

As you navigate any milestone day, whether it is one that is collectively acknowledged or one more private to your own journey, allow yourself to create breathing room. Put multiple plans in place. Communicate these with the people in your life. Allow them to choose in or out. Give yourself permission to pick what you need, not what you think you are supposed to do or what you feel (internal or external) pressure to do.

And remember, there is no perfect way of getting through—just strategies and support to do the best we can, one day at a time.

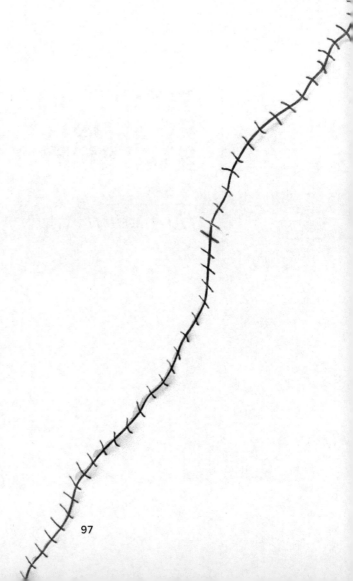

TOXIC POSITIVITY STATEMENT

"_____ got through it, you will too!"

Release: *Comparing.*

Non-Response: Smile and re-direct or end conversation (smiling is optional)

Boundaried Response: Please don't compare me or my experience to _____.

Educating Response: I love you for wanting to help me and remind me that I will get through this. I know that I will. And what would really support me, which I know is your goal, is not comparing me to anyone else. We don't know all that they went through and my own experience is completely unique. The only way to get through The only way to get through it is to GO through it, and I would love for you to support me in being with me in the hard and painful part of being in it right now.

Reframe: This person is showing their love in a way that doesn't serve me. They want to remind me that they believe in me. I have the ability to choose to see their love and intent and help them direct it in a way that results in a more supportive and progressive impact. I know that I have the ability to get through this and I allow it to be really challenging right now.

CHAPTER **7**

Enlisting Support:
A SACRED AND NECESSARY PROCESS

One evening when visiting my parents, I ran down to the basement to see the new wine cellar. Next to the bottles of red I was so excited to choose from was Leyden's nursery—well, all the items from it that had been packed away and stored. It had been too painful for me to pack up her nursery, to take down the room that represented the future I had envisioned. So being the incredible Teammates that they are, my family went to my home and gently packed away each one of Leyden's New England Patriots onesies, never worn holiday dresses, endless children's books, and the decor I had spent hours choosing, to make sure it was perfect, for Leyden. I hadn't thought about where all the items were being stored. Ready or not, I was now looking at them.

I felt the tsunami of tears building somewhere from deep inside, it was as if that tide had also taken my breath away with it. I couldn't breathe, I couldn't speak, I couldn't move. I stood there frozen in time just like Leyden's time capsule of items. Items I had shopped for, or her grandparents had made for her. The earthy toned shades of green and beige were everywhere. *My life was supposed to be this.* Well, maybe not so neat and tidy and with more diapers and throw up everywhere, but Leyden's stuff didn't belong here. It belonged with me, in our home, in her nursery.

While we can learn how to navigate our grief, our losses, our challenges with all the tools in the world, we are not meant to do so alone.

Society glorifies the struggle.

We love the underdog in stories, movies, sports, and music. We embrace the idea of earning a donut through a tough workout, being worthy of financial freedom from the hustle, and there is an unspoken stigma around asking for help—as if help is weakness.

Admittedly, prior to losing Leyden I was resistant to asking for help proactively. I had to wait for things to get really bad to ask for support. Or worse, I would consistently put myself into situations where I only had myself to depend on. I would force myself to not have the option to get help, simply because I didn't know how to ask. And in some way or shape, I would act out the very unmet needs that I had deprived myself of getting met. Grief is lonely, isolating, and overwhelming.

We don't need to make it lonelier by trying to manage it on our own.

While we explored different types of Teammates, it's also important to be aware of different depths and capacities our Teammates have as well.

The phone calls to my "listener" friends couldn't go on forever. They have lives, families, jobs, and their own emotional health to take care of.

The requests for my "distractors" to entertain me also couldn't go on forever either.

Asking for Support

Grief teaches us how to be really clear on what we need, where we can access that, and how to ask for specific types of support we need.

After the exchange with the flustered parent, now leaving me flustered, I knew I needed to ask for support.

I walked to my boss's office and asked for a few minutes.

He made time, and I explained what happened.

There were two truths here: We were probably going to have to do some follow-up and cleanup with the parent to avoid political backlash or a slew of posts about it on local town news websites (welcome to the world of education). And I needed some time, space, and support to manage the deep pain I was feeling of having "not being a mother" thrown in my face just four months after I held my daughter for her last breath.

I agreed to write my own email to the parent and asked for his support if any further meetings or calls were needed.

He compassionately reminded me that yes, we have a job to do, and yes, I get to have support, and there was nothing wrong with that.

Support beyond working needs was required. I could call on my Teammates of course, but solely depending on our friends and family to support us is not sustainable, or truthfully, in full responsibility for our emotional needs.

In addition to my Teammates, I had enlisted an army of support.

I:

Was a member of a bereaved parents' group at the hospital.

Hired a grief counselor.

Worked with a therapist.

Had a life mentor/coach.

Joined a local chapter of grief support for people managing all types of grief.

Regularly met with my Reverend.

If none of these professionals were available, I created a library of books, podcasts, and videos that provided research or experience-driven support.

Creating Your Toolbox

In addition to the support, I built a "toolbox" of things I could do on my own to self-soothe including crying, punching pillows, running, doing yoga, writing, looking at photos or videos, going for a walk, or sleeping.

While many people encouraged meditation and dance, modalities that could be very effective for you, for me, they were just inaccessible at that time. Meditation turned into racing thoughts and more anxiety. It wasn't until later on in my healing that I found meditation and dance movements to help me

Weekends for those in the depths of grief mean loneliness. While the world is crashing in on you, it seems to continue to spin as normal for everyone else. They just continue on with their lives, something at that very moment you may feel completely incapable of doing. This is where your toolbox becomes your greatest ally.

As you build your own toolbox, bring an awareness around which "tools" actually support you. Do not feel pressure to put a certain tool in there because you saw it on social media, or it worked for someone else. We will talk about how comparison stunts your healing in grief in more depth in a later chapter. For now, allow yourself to grant permission to be authentic and true about what will truly support. Here are some examples of tools that I have used or supported clients in using:

- *painting*
- *singing*
- *dancing*
- *meditating*
- *breathwork*

- *journaling/writing*
- *boxing*
- *batting cage*
- *hot/cold therapy*
- *long walks*
- *podcasts*
- *books*
- *talk therapy*
- *float tanks*
- *hiking*
- *sitting in silence*
- *support groups*
- *one-on-one coaches*
- *hosting charity events*
- *exercising*
- *arts/crafts/scrapbooking*
- *cooking or baking*

Strengthening the Scar Tissue

Write out a toolbox of ten to fifteen ideas to support yourself when unanticipated triggers present. Keep it simple. While we can have multiple game plans and Teammates in place for a difficult day or event, preparing ourselves for the inevitable, unanticipated triggers is critical to the healing process.

You are Worthy of Support

The truth is, when that woman said, "You wouldn't know; you aren't a mother," it crushed me. But because my capacity was limited, it didn't just crush me, it took me out.

The societal pressures to figure it all out on our own create breakdown when we wait too long to seek help. The key is seeking support proactively, when we are at eighty percent of our limit, not at one hundred percent of our limit.

Noticing that I had no emotional space to manage my responsibilities, and there were things that needed to be managed, I sought support from my boss. We explored how my role was requiring me to hold space for the mother more than I could at that time and that he was able and willing to do so. Ultimately, the woman who entered my office, though it wasn't necessarily an effective or fair way to do so, needed me to listen, allow her to vent, and to feel as though I was on her team. She wasn't looking for a dosage of mindset and emotional intelligence training I gave her. I also called a Teammate, one who could listen without interjecting and talking negatively about the woman or advising me on how to manage it, but rather, just listen to me cry and hold space for my pain. And beyond that, I called my therapist and scheduled an additional appointment from what we already had.

The idea of doing it on our own is not only antiquated, it's a recipe to contribute to breeding instability, overwhelm, loneliness, and thoughts of wanting to give up.

The courage is asking for support before things fall apart.

The challenge is in knowing our worthiness in doing so—and letting go of society's glorification of each of us trying to be a hero and muscle through.

Asking for support isn't easy. I have worked with a number of clients who cognitively understand that doing so is important, but when it comes to speaking the words or sending the text, they freeze.

If asking for support is a challenge for you, here are some ways that you can do so:

- This is hard for me to ask, would you be able to _____?
- It would really support me to have _____.
- Is there a time you are free to talk? I could use some support.
- If you are open to it, _____.
- I really need _____. Is that something you are able to help me with?

When you do stretch outside of your comfort zone and ask for support, or open up and share the messy, raw, parts of you, prepare yourself for a vulnerability hangover. You may find yourself replaying what you said, wondering if you overshared, and feeling completely yucky and exposed. This is normal! And the good news is that with time, it becomes easier. Like a workout, endurance training, being a parent, driving a car... It all becomes easier and natural with time and repetition. Build that vulnerability muscle by choosing into it. And allocate for some rest and recovery time afterward.

GLIMMER OF GOLD
Asking for help is different than asking for someone to fix you.

Types of Triggers

Last chapter we spoke about how to put your Teammates and plans A, B, C, and D in place. This is critical for when you are facing what I call "anticipated triggers." Anticipated triggers are things such as holidays, anniversaries, events, or gatherings where you can predict or anticipate discomfort and support that is needed to navigate it.

But, we also have to understand "unanticipated triggers." These are things such as the parent who told me I wasn't a mother, a commercial you may see, a song you may hear, or anything else unanticipated that can evoke the pain and loss that you have within.

For years I have told my clients, "You can't suddenly use a new tool when sh*t hits the fan; you are going to reach for a tool that you trust and are used to."

What I mean by this is that when things get tough, your nervous system isn't going to allow you to suddenly start practicing a new tool such as meditation, if you have never meditated. This is why proactively putting new tools and practices in place is critical. We can only work with what we are comfortable working with. This is also why so many people have a hard time breaking cycles of unhealthy coping. If we cope by lashing out, numbing out, or tuning out, unless we are intentionally sourcing other ways to manage our emotional flare-ups, when the trigger comes, those will be the only ways that we continue to work through it.

Unanticipated triggers can take us out because we don't see them coming. I'll never forget, one evening as I was feeling down, I decided to purchase a new pair of sneakers to get back into running, as something to do for myself in a positive way of healing. I logged onto Amazon as I always do, and immediately, my breath was taken from me.

"Items left in your cart..."

"Based on your shopping history..."

"Inspired by your purchase..."

Suddenly, my computer was filled with the items I had "saved for later" for Leyden's nursery. A set of sage green curtains, a color to match the earthy tones of her room, a set of baby shoes, newborn onesies, and some summer outfits that spoke "beach baby" for anticipation for when Leyden would get to fall in love with the ocean like her mother. Tears streamed down my face uncontrollably as I began yelling, "I want my baby back! I am so sorry, Leyden; I am so sorry."

While many triggers are anticipated, a majority are unanticipated. For me, it was the "do you have any children?" questions and not knowing how to answer, and my grandmother, who suffered from dementia, asking me, "Where is your baby?" Maybe it was a song I heard that was on her playlist, seeing another big blue-eyed infant at a restaurant, watching the "first day of school" photos fill Facebook...I don't know how I would have gotten through what felt like gut punch after gut punch without not only the tools I had built for myself, but the supports I had put in place to help me.

When we intentionally seek support, we are coming from a place of courage, responsibility, and performing the greatest act of self-love we can.

In turn, it's selfless.

It allows us to then have more capacity and clarity to show up for other people in our lives.

There is nothing weak or selfish about that.

TOXIC POSITIVITY STATEMENT

"Just think positive..."

Release: Shame for having emotions perceived as negative.

Responses:

Non-Response: Smile and re-direct or end conversation (smiling is optional)

Boundaried Response: I don't find that approach to be healthy for the long-term processing of painful experiences.

Educating Response: If I do that, I am stuffing down my truth and that could result in me exploding or show up in my physical health. I appreciate you seeking to support me, but the best way is to help me think progressively which includes embracing and working through the reality of emotions I have right now.

Reframe: There are no "right" or "wrong" feelings—these are all part of the human experience of feeling—and that is sacred. I discern between dwelling in the negative and allowing the painful to exist. I choose progressive over forcing positive feelings that I do not feel.

CHAPTER **8**

Ways We Stay Stuck:

FILLING YOUR EMOTIONAL BANK ACCOUNT

And just like that, the "shoulds" creep in.

It was the end of October, and I was packing for a weekend-long event in New York where I would be a guest speaker for a group of entrepreneurs.

Out of nowhere, it hit me.

I shouldn't be doing this.

I should be taking care of Leyden.

I should be picking out a Halloween costume.

And if she was anything like me: *I should be checking under her bed for pre-holiday candy wrappers.*

It continued.

I shouldn't know half of what I know and teach—because they are all things that I learned and lived through Leyden's death.

The shoulds got louder. *THIS NEVER SHOULD HAVE HAPPENED.*

Her case never should have been the catastrophe it was termed.

Suddenly, the packing excitement turned into uncontrollable tears.

Everything in me was boiling over, as though I had forgotten about a pot on the burning stove. I had let the rage and anger simmer. It was inevitably going to boil over, over into my life, my career, my friendships. That rage had a hold on me that I had yet to realize.

The roller coaster of grief is extreme.

Sure entrepreneurship, raising a family, and living life all come with roller coaster waves.

Grief intensifies them, massively.

During our grief journey, we can enlist support to build our world—not to make grief smaller but to allow the percentage of the space our loss consumes to be less. Within the ecosystem of our Teammates and our external activities, communities, and connections, we find ourselves at the center.

And we cannot forget the importance of our thoughts and words we choose—as they become our reality.

Imagine you are holding a cup of water.

And in that cup, the water represents your happiness, fulfillment, peace.

Most people are always chasing MORE to pour in the cup.

But in this chapter, I am going to show you how you don't need MORE. You do not need more money, more friends, more followers on social media, or money in your bank account to feel better. Imagine that all of those things were additional water you are pouring into your cup. So let's just say that you pour in more.

You stay up late, work weekends, get on a dating app...whatever it is.

You spend all of your energy chasing MORE.

And, perhaps, as a result of that, you are pouring more into that cup.

But here's the problem. Most people spend their time and energy chasing more rather than closing the holes that are leaking. If that cup of yours has holes in it, you can pour in all the water you want, but you are just going to exhaust yourself—as if you are running in circles to find the fulfillment you desire, but no matter what you do, how much you make, where you travel to, you still don't feel what you are desiring to feel.

So rather than chasing more, can we look at where we are leaking out what we already have?

The best part about this is, it alleviates the pressure to chase, force, or do more.

The hardest part about this is, unlearning behavior or habits takes a lot of time, intention, and commitment.

The biggest holes in our cups tend to be unhealed wounds and our default thoughts. Grief will beg you to heal any unhealed wound and strengthen your mindset. Because you can't afford to be leaking out energy when you are running on empty, and getting through each day feels exhausting in itself.

Releasing the "Shoulds"

For me, I found that if I was going to make it through my grief without staying stuck in the past, I needed to teach myself, to literally train my brain, to detach from the word "should." Otherwise, this six-letter word was going to drown me in emptiness, longing, and pain.

Having studied neuro-linguistic programming and gotten a master's degree in education focusing on language-based learning, I knew just how important words are.

In order to feel better, I had to feel differently.

To feel differently, I had to think differently.

To think differently, I needed to intentionally train my thoughts almost as strategically as if I were training my body for a marathon.

The reality in grief is that after some time, the sympathy cards stop coming in. People forget. They don't see the broken heart. Or some who never met you have no freaking clue that you are carrying the weight of the world inside.

And that's perfectly okay.

It would have been unrealistic to expect everyone to accommodate my feelings and pain each day.

So understanding energy and being in charge of what I did and didn't take on was literally my flotation device during a time when I felt like I was drowning.

Remember, energy can't be created or destroyed, but it can be transformed.

Power in Our Words

One of the ways that we can shift our energy is to look at the words that we are using and begin choosing words that support us. Like all parts of our grief journey, it starts within before we look out.

Notice here where you can replace certain words and phrases with alternatives that better support you in growing through your grief rather than being powerless to it.

It's important to remember that this is a choice.

And it doesn't lessen or devalue the depths of what you are navigating and carrying.

It doesn't call upon toxic positivity or dismissing the pain.

GLIMMER OF GOLD

Courage lies in the coexistence of the reality and pain we carry alongside the willingness to heal through it.

As we begin to shift our internal and external dialogue, the lens through which we witness our experiences shifts. Our words and our thoughts are always in alignment. And as we go deeper, this leads to our actions.

LADDER ACTIVITY

*your partner/friend/colleague/
family members ladder of priorities*

your ladder of priorities

Remember that actions always come from a thought or an energy dynamic that is driving that thought. When we commit to this energy or thought, it will drive what we see and as a result, drive what we do.

Strengthening the Scar Tissue

Choose one word that stands out to you and commit to replacing it for the next forty-eight hours in both internal and external dialogue.

One of the easiest ways I coach this concept is what I call the "red car method."

Truth be told, I have had a lot of cars.

Driving isn't my forte; in fact, I hate it.

Many times, I wonder if my guardian angels are intervening through vehicles to let me know when I need to surrender, slow down, check something in my world, or find a new path to travel.

Regardless, when I got a new car (which has been many times), I noticed that suddenly everyone else bought the same car too!

Imagine if you just bought a brand new car—your dream car.

You shopped around, did your research, and finally landed on the perfect choice for what you want to drive.

If you can't think of a new car or a dream car, just imagine that you bought a red car, for example.

So often when we get our new car, or that new red car, driving down the backroads, in parking lots, or on the highway, you suddenly notice that so many other people have red cars too!

The reality isn't that at the same exact time you purchased a new vehicle, people all around ran to purchase the same one or same color— it's because your attention is more focused on your car, and where your attention is focused internally, you find that in the outer world.

Where energy goes, energy grows.

Through my work with thousands of individuals in varying capacities, I have found that there are eight primary ways in which our humanness can do its human thing, and we find ourselves stuck.

We are constantly collecting evidence of the stories we tell ourselves.

So, let's examine the stories (or energies) that can keep our vehicles in park:

1. SHOULDING: "Shoulding" is a term used to describe a cognitive distortion or unhelpful thinking pattern where individuals impose unrealistic expectations or demands on themselves or others. It involves using the words "should" or "shouldn't" when thinking about how things ought to be or how one should behave. "Shoulding" often leads to feelings of guilt, self-criticism, and inadequacy when one feels unable to meet these self-imposed or external expectations.

2. COMPARISON: Comparison is the act of assessing or evaluating oneself, others, or situations by comparing them with others or an idealized standard. It can involve comparing achievements, appearance, possessions, or life circumstances, among other things. Comparison can sometimes lead to feelings of envy, inadequacy, or low self-esteem if individuals perceive themselves as falling short in comparison to others.

3. FORCE: Force refers to the act of compelling or coercing someone to do something against their will or without their consent. It involves using physical strength, authority, or power to exert control over others or situations. In some cases, force may also refer to the imposition of pressure or influence to achieve a particular outcome.

4. AVOIDANCE: Avoidance is a coping mechanism where individuals intentionally evade or steer clear of certain situations, emotions, or responsibilities they find distressing or uncomfortable. We can avoid a number of ways—through avoiding conversations, going to certain places, or avoiding feeling things through numbing out with substances, binging TV shows or movies, or avoiding by scrolling for hours on social media.

5. EXPECTATIONS: Expectations are beliefs or assumptions individuals hold about the way things should or will happen in the future. These beliefs can be about themselves, others, or circumstances. Expectations can influence emotions and behavior, and unmet expectations may lead to disappointment or frustration.

6. VICTIMIZATION: Victimization refers to the perception or belief that one is a victim of circumstances, events, or other people's actions. It involves adopting a mindset of powerlessness and attributing negative outcomes to external factors, often without acknowledging one's role or responsibility in the situation.

7. CATASTROPHIZING: Catastrophizing is a cognitive distortion where individuals tend to magnify the significance of negative events or potential outcomes, imagining the worst possible scenario. They may assume that a minor setback will lead to disastrous consequences, leading to increased anxiety and stress.

8. LACKING OR MISUSING BOUNDARIES: Lacking boundaries refers to a situation where individuals have difficulty establishing and maintaining clear personal limits and may struggle to assert themselves in interpersonal relationships. This can lead to feeling overwhelmed, taken advantage of, or emotionally drained by others' demands and expectations. Misusing boundaries is when we assert a boundary but really instead of a healthy boundary, it is avoiding, hiding, or even gaslighting.

MIND DETOX
Release limiting thought patterns

- **Should/have to:** *Get to, choosing to, want to, opportunity to*
- **It will get better when:** *I can take action now by*
- **Must be nice:** *If I really wanted to I could, I wonder how they achieved that*
- **A least/but:** *Nothing or use the word and*
- **Don't forget:** *I will remember, let's make a point to*
- **Why is this happening to me:** *I wonder why it's happening to me*
- **Gossip/disaster stories:** *Just stop*
- **Everyone/always:** *Be specific. Who/when/what is actually fact*
- **Complains:** *Gratitude*
- **Regret/guilt/shame:** *Letting go, trust, grownth*
- **Assumption:** *A hundred stories could be true*
- **I don't have time/I can't:** *It's not a priority, I am not making time*

If you aren't sure how these may or may not be present in your life, that's okay. What we are doing is removing ourselves from being on autopilot, as most of our thoughts and actions come from autopilot. We are pausing, observing, and giving ourselves the space to see if we are choosing from a place of growth or choosing from a place that will keep us stuck.

Social Media Check-Up

While there are many ways to begin to observe if and how these energies present in your life, one of the easiest places to observe if these are present in your world is through social media.

Social media has revolutionized communication, enabling people from around the world to engage and stay informed in real time. Like it or not, it has become the primary way in which much of our world shares, expresses, and connects.

I have coached hundreds of entrepreneurs, and almost every single one of them has found breakthroughs in their life by looking at their relationship with social media.

Jessica was afraid to post about her business because she thought people would think she was an imposter. She literally stayed up at night with thoughts about how people would judge her, talk about her photo or video, and had visions of friends or family sitting together and gossiping about what she was doing. Jessica was catastrophizing. We focused on the reality of what was happening and also shifted into the possibility that people could be inspired by what she shared.

Lisa struggled to make decisions because she was looking at what everyone else was doing, and instead of trusting and creating her own process, she would try to imitate someone else's. She found herself changing her mind all the time or switching to what was working for someone else. When we looked deeper, we saw that comparison was holding her back in many aspects of her life. By breaking through it in how she related to social media, she was able to break through it in how she compared to other people's bodies, relationships, careers, and more.

Joe was discouraged when he shared about a workshop he was hosting, and no one signed up. When we assessed it, we saw that he had only shared it two times. He had an expectation that he was going to suddenly announce something new, and people were going to rush to work with him. This provided the landscape to look at where his expectations in general were impacting his life and how he could attach more to the process of consistency, connecting, and being true to himself and detach from an expectation of a certain outcome by a certain deadline.

Steve found himself saying things like, "Must be nice," when he would see other people's vacations, family photos, or achievements online. This victimization energy was disempowering him from owning his own possibility and focusing on what he could create instead of harboring resentment for what others created.

In all of these examples, change started with awareness. But awareness isn't enough.

What I discovered in supporting individuals is the awareness of these things, without further action steps, can bring feelings of shame, embarrassment, or thoughts of, *What is wrong with me?*

Strengthening the Scar Tissue

Focus on bringing awareness to thoughts that may be keeping you stuck or perhaps feeling like you are on an emotional hamster wheel. Start a list in your phone, journal, or notebook. Awareness is a building block for change, and it's important to simply become aware of thoughts that do not serve well. You will revisit this list soon when it is time to take action to break free of these.

In a later chapter, I will show you the four-step method I developed, after working with so many clients, to take them from awareness of something that was not serving them, to releasing and replacing this with a new thought, behavior, or choice. From this method, hundreds of individuals have undone years or decades of autopilot decision-making to find growth and freedom in their life.

The truth? Most people feel more comfortable when you're broken. Why? Because your light doesn't challenge their darkness. Your ambition doesn't question their comfort.

Your healing doesn't force them to look at their own wounds. It's a sad reality, but here's the good news—the people who are meant for you, your real people, will love you at every stage. Broken, mending, thriving. They'll celebrate your wins, not envy them. They'll root for your growth, not resent it.

And they'll stand with you, not just when you're down, but especially when you rise.

Don't dim your light to make others more comfortable. You weren't made to stay broken. You were made to shine bright like a diamond.

TOXIC POSITIVITY STATEMENT

"Look on the bright side..."

Release: *Ignoring the pain.*

Responses:

Non-Response: Smile and re-direct or end conversation (smiling is optional)

Boundaried Response: I am not in a place right now where that feels supportive.

Educating Response: I want to help you in supporting me, and when you say that, I feel like I am not allowed to be honest about how I am feeling which is going to make me pull away from you. If my pain is too heavy for you, I won't rely on you to process it with and that is OK, but please don't dismiss it or try to get me to ignore it.

Reframe: There is a duality and coexistence that is unavoidable. In fact, the duality is beautiful. The darker the dark, the lighter the light on the other side of it. It is a process, and the only way is to move through it in my own way, at my own pace.

PART THREE

GETTING REALLY REAL

There is nothing more *lonely* than
being *surrounded* by people who
don't know what you're carrying.
It's a different kind of lonely. Not the kind
when you are physically alone. The kind
where you're surrounded by people and still
feel unseen. Because they don't know
what you're carrying. They don't see *the*
weight behind the smile.

CHAPTER 9

Scatterplotting Your Life:

RELATIONSHIP RIPPLES AND SECONDARY LOSSES

"What are the other losses that you can think of?" she asked me.

Annoyed, I peered up through my swollen eyes.

It was hard enough to get myself out of the house and to her office. Now, she was going to waste my time talking to me about "other losses."

Before I could respond, my grief counselor continued. "What losses related to Leyden are you experiencing that aren't the direct loss of Leyden but are layers of grief related to her loss?"

The first thing that came to my mind brought me to hysterics.

I remembered how Leyden looked at her uncle TJ in awe, wanting nothing to do with me when he visited, and imagining her growing up looking up in adoration to my brothers, her three handsome uncles. My mother debated over whether she preferred "Nonny" or "Grammy." Those moments all came rushing back to me in one fell swoop. I never got to witness Leyden growing up with her uncles, Nonny, and Poppy. I would never hear her laugh as her uncles chased her through a blanket and pillow fort. I was mourning these other losses as well and had never realized it until that very moment.

"Seeing my brothers as uncles, and my parents as grandparents." I could barely finish my sentence.

But I understood where she was guiding me.

Part of healing is untangling grief—untangling all the layers and emotions that we place in one space. And when we do that, it can feel so overwhelming to manage or heal that we stop, "wait for it to get better," or think it's impossible.

However, when we begin to see the entire ecosystem of our grief as many little entities that contribute to the primary pain, it can be easier to dedicate time and energy to one smaller space than to the whole.

Think of what losses you are enduring as a result of the initial loss.

Unfortunately, when you check one grief box off the list, there are more that follow.

Perhaps if you are navigating a divorce, you are not only grieving the relationship but the family dynamic, mutual friends, holiday traditions, and more.

Or if you are grieving a miscarriage, you are also carrying the dreams of what could have been, a sibling for another child, seeing your parents as grandparents, or the future envisioned.

The impact and power of secondary losses is widely misunderstood, and because of this, our pain is confused or compounded. I want to untangle as much of the messiness with you as possible so that you can alleviate any unnecessary pain.

It's an important distinction to recognize that we cannot eliminate the pain directly related to our grief, but we can eliminate pain from the confusion that can swirl around it.

PRIMARY   SECONDARY

Loss of future envisioned
Loss of family dynamic
Loss of seeing others as
grandparents, aunts,
uncles and more
Loss of friendships
Loss of financial envisioned
Loss of life/loved one   *Loss of trust/security*
End of a relationship,   *Loss of traditions*
Loss of sense of self   *Loss of hope*
Los of sense of humor
Loss of happiness
Loss of meaning
Loss of feelings of safety
Loss of faith/religious beliefs
Loss of a "unit"
Loss of future memories

Secondary losses are those that exist because of your primary loss. So often we focus on the primary loss and neglect all the "smaller" ones. The truth is, they aren't that small, and they do add up. When assessing secondary losses, think of what else you feel you are "missing" as a result of your primary loss.

In addition to the loss of seeing my brothers as uncles and my parents as grandparents, I felt a deep secondary loss of experiencing motherhood with all my best friends who were also moms. We had spent Leyden's last day out of the hospital together with our babies. Our group chats had shifted from college talk to dating, weddings, and now children. I didn't know how I would belong again.

The actual act of being a mother was a loss secondary to the loss of Leyden.

There is no need to identify all of your secondary losses at once, as they will slowly present when you feel a "pang" pulling at you. The best thing to do is simply educate yourself on the concept of secondary losses and start noting when they present for you so that you can tend to them separately from tending to your primary loss. Write them down, keep a note on your phone, or share them out loud. By identifying them and treating them as a separate entity, you are better prepared to manage your emotional responses to the very real pain you feel.

One Moment at a Time

Many times, we will avoid the spaces that trigger these secondary losses. It took me a long time to be able to be around my friends and their babies. All I saw was what I was missing; the future of our kids growing up together and holding an infant, when all I wanted was mine back, was just too much. And seeing my grandmother, whom Leyden was named after, I also avoided. I couldn't manage the loss of facing the woman I admired so much that I named my daughter after her and not ever being able to witness my nana hold her namesake, Leyden.

While there is an element to protecting and honoring our needs, it's important for us to remember that there is a tipping point, one that only we know, where we are actually compounding our losses and creating more loss by avoiding the triggers. The reality is, when we avoid the friendships, vacation sites, family members, venues, churches, and more that remind us of what is missing, we are also creating distance between ourselves and the very places that we love that at some point could create and provide healing, comfort, and love. The first time I held an infant, I cried while smiling. Surrounded by my immediate and extended family, I braced myself for the pain, sat on the couch, and asked to hold my godson, Carter Leyden. Sometimes medicine is painful, uncomfortable, and triggering. Yet it can still be medicine. As he stared back at me, without any idea of what that moment meant, I healed a new layer.

The most important thing we can do is one moment at a time, bring aware-ness to our needs, and a little bit at a time, bring awareness to our grief—the layers, the primary and secondary losses, the triggers.

Shifting Relationships

A secondary loss that is harder to talk about is the loss of relationships. But I am not just talking about an actual splitting of ways. Many times after the loss of a loved one—parent, pet, child, family member, friend—couples can find that the relationship shifts in a way that they feel a grief and mourning for what it used to be but struggle to articulate what is wrong as the relationship remains intact. Rather than a secondary loss, as the partnership is still there, I think of this as "relationship ripples." The grief can have a ripple effect on our most sig-nificant and intimate relationships.

What I learned is that while the stigma is that relationships end when there is massive trauma or loss that impacts the couple or family, it's not necessari-ly statistically higher than the average American divorce rate. In my studies, I learned that relationships end not necessarily from the loss itself but from the expectations of others to navigate the loss the same way that you do.

Distraught in my grief counselor's office, I so badly wanted to make my partner wrong for the ways in which he was managing the loss. This was com-pounded by the comments I would get from people around me asking how he was taking care of me, what he was doing, if he was helping me heal. I was so caught up in my own grief, my own needs, that when I heard this perspective, I realized that I was falling into societal stigmas that say one person (typically the male or masculine) is responsible for navigating grief the way the female (or feminine) does.

I sat in silence for a little while, thinking of that sentence over and over:

"The expectation for the person to navigate it the same way that you do..."

What was my expectation?

In truth, I wanted to be saved, taken care of.

While all I wanted to do was sleep with Leyden's things, look at her pic-tures, and talk about the loss as I processed, Leyden's father had very real and different needs. Space, alone time, being in the woods, being with his own fami-ly members—that brought him solace and healing. Looking at me and looking at Leyden's things was painful for him. Meanwhile, clinging to him, the closest link I had to Leyden, was healing for me.

Was one of us right or wrong?

Who was going to have to sacrifice our unique, differing, and real needs?

Strengthening the Scar Tissue

My therapist took me through an activity that I want to invite you into. If you feel as though anyone in your life is not navigating the loss in the way you want or expect them to, pause for a moment and try this out.

Go ahead and draw two ladders next to each other. They each need about four to five rungs. Label one ladder as yours and one as the other person in your life. Now list from top to bottom what is the most important or urgent thing in each of your lives. For me, rungs one, two, and three were all around Leyden. For Leyden's father, they were different. Different doesn't mean better or worse. It just means something different.

What this taught me was a new level of personal responsibility and ownership in navigating my grief—a level that I didn't want and was tempted to fight but one that I knew was only up to me to truly heal and find my way again.

If I chose to spend my time and energy convincing the people I was the closest to that I needed them to, I was putting my energy in a place that wasn't serving me.

Take a moment to pause.

No matter what your grief is, whether it is a break-up, empty nest, loss of a loved one, pet, miscarriage, infertility, moving, or something else, how much energy are you putting into meeting your own needs? How much energy are you putting into seeking others to meet your own needs? And how much energy are you putting into judging or watching how someone else is navigating the same loss?

We don't pause to make it wrong. We pause to bring awareness, to learn. So that from the pause, we can choose what is truly going to honor ourselves and the people we care about.

GLIMMER OF GOLD
Different doesn't mean better or worse. It just means something different.

As we explored the concept of Teammates in an earlier chapter, using the ladder when looking at your Team will support you in remembering that other people in your life are navigating their own busy lives too. This doesn't mean we cannot ask for or seek support; it simply alleviates any hidden expectation of everyone in our lives to stop their life because of what we are navigating. It shifts from a place of disappointment that we are not getting "more support" to gratitude for the support we are receiving.

There will be ripples in your relationships through your grief journey. One of my clients said to me that I helped her learn that any time she wants to change or grow into new versions of herself, there will be elements of grief internally as well as in the relationships around her. Inevitably, as we change, our relationships change. That brings grief.

Our Changing Paths

Think of your life like a scatterplot. Each dot represents a different path you are on or phase you are experiencing. Sometimes the dot can be high up, sometimes very low, and of course, anywhere in between. You can literally draw out (or simply visualize) your scatterplot. See your path going all over the place; perhaps you thought you were headed in one direction and then suddenly you are somewhere completely different.

Now, think of someone else's scatterplot. What would theirs look like next to yours? If you took the lines for you and someone in your life, where would they intersect? Where would they be tracking closely? Where would there be major gaps?

If we are all inevitably on our own scatterplot, it is reasonable to remember that letting go of the expectation of others to abandon their path to join us on ours isn't setting ourselves up to strengthen our relationships. In fact, in seeking and desiring connection, this could actually create more distance if someone feels like they are not enough, or the pressure is just too heavy, so they avoid. The reality is that your relationships will have ripples in them from your grief. The deeper the grief, the wider the ripples. Some relationships will strengthen. Some will fade away. Some will need space before strengthening. Some will bring clarity that this relationship is no longer serving you. Allowing these truths rather than clinging to what was will provide freedom in not only your grief journey but your life.

Riding the Ripples

The best tool to navigate these ripples is effectively communicating with curiosity, patience, and by listening. As humans with complex minds, we will often create stories around our experiences to try to make sense of them. For example, one of my closest friends, who had a child just a few weeks older than Leyden, avoided talking to me about her daughter, and in general, our conversations were less frequent. I learned with time that she was really struggling with sleepless nights as a new mom. The fatigue and frustration, the grief of the life she knew, was real for her. Yet she felt shame around bringing it up to me, as if because I had been through something so much worse, she was wrong to feel the way she did. When we talked about this, not only did it source more connection and understanding, it stopped what felt like a scratch in our relationship from becoming a wound.

Comparing and understanding are very different. Comparing to others from a place of right or wrong, better or worse will create massive divides in relationships. Understanding the different experiences and honoring the truth to all of them can strengthen bonds in even the most painful times.

I remember growing up hearing the phrase in so many settings: "You need to finish your plate; there are starving children in _____ (insert country)." It brought a guilt or shame that because someone was struggling, I had to do something that I didn't want to do, or I was not grateful. As I got older, I used this example with many of my clients fighting comparison or guilt around their experiences and explained it to them like this: It is my job to be responsible and resourceful for how much food I do or do not take. I can also contribute funds or support to campaigns and charities that support communities lacking access to food and water. But it's not my job to have a stomachache because someone else in the world is hungry. My stomachache isn't going to help their hunger. Stuffing down your pain because someone has it "worse" is not going to help their healing.

As you choose to heal, you will find that reengaging with places that were a trigger can actually become medicine, over time. After spending most nights listening to the ocean waves on the white noise app with Leyden to calm her and quiet out any hospital beeping, I couldn't go to the ocean for quite some time. It was too big, vast, and reminded me of the one day I did take her to the beach when we were home. Now, on my most painful days, I find solace, reprieve, and new levels of life and breath from visiting the ocean. It means so much to me, I moved to be a bike ride away from it. Note that the ocean has never changed; the way I relate to it did.

When focusing on your own healing, you can discover new levels of self-love through awareness of your needs that can truly change your life. I must be honest, however, and caution against the thinking that can stop both of these things from happening. The too often said, "It will get better when," is not going to heal the pain. Find the courage to do the deep work, gently, to take ownership of your healing rather than passing it off to time. The only thing time provides is the space to do the work. It's up to each of us to choose it.

TOXIC POSITIVITY STATEMENT

"God only gives you what you can handle…"

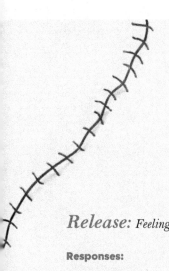

Release: *Feeling like you asked for it or invited it.*

Responses:

Non-Response: Smile and re-direct or end conversation (smiling is optional)

Boundaried Response: That doesn't resonate with me right now, but thank you.

Educating Response: When you say that I feel like I asked for this or I am being taught a lesson which makes me feel more heaviness, shame and confusion. It would be most supportive if you could remind me that you believe in my strength and are here to support me because no matter how strong I am, this is really hard.

Reframe: I can honor and acknowledge my strength without feeling pressure to not be hurting and in pain. Being strong doesn't mean I do not feel, it means that I can trust in my ability to get through and not ignore, stifle or dismiss the challenge of doing so. I was not given anything to be punished, and I trust all of this is happening for me in some way that I cannot see right now.

CHAPTER 10

The Whack-a-Mole Game:

CALLING BULLSH*T ON GOOD VIBES ONLY

When I was a kid, I loved going to Chuck E. Cheese. Pizza, soda, and arcade games? Yes, please. I would spend hours strategizing to see which games would provide the most return on investment. Meaning, which ones did I have the best chance at winning the most tickets? This way I could have a better shot at the top shelf prizes at the Chuck E. Cheese prize booth. One of my favorite games to play was whack-a-mole. You know that game where the little mole popped up, and you had to quickly react and knock it down? But before you knew it, it was popping up somewhere ELSE again.

Years later, okay, maybe decades, I can't think of that game without associating it with my grief. Not because I planned to take Leyden there. Truth be told, I vowed I never would. But because grief is a lot like whack-a-mole.

Our society teaches us to "push down" grief due to the uncomfortable nature of the emotional experience. Social media is plagued with "just think positive" or "good vibes only." I call bullshit on that. Not only do I call bullshit, I will go as far as to say that this way of thinking massively disservices humanity, the emotional experience, and our ability to cope with it.

It adds shame and guilt as if there were something wrong with us for feeling sad, angry, resentful, or bitter. The beauty of the emotional experience is that we experience all the emotions. The work is in navigating them in a way that moves us forward, at whatever pace on whatever path that may be.

Unlike whack-a-mole, where we are the only ones with the mallet knocking down the mole, people all around us are holding their own mallets.

"I don't know how I am going to get through this," we say.

"It will get better when..." (WHACK) we hear.

"I can't get out of bed," we share.

"Think positive, at least you have_____" (WHACK).

Perpetual positivity can actually be a form of denial and avoidance of the emotional experience.

Stuffing down our feelings, or others stuffing them down, is an unwinnable game of whack-a-mole.

Knock it down in one place; it'll come up again somewhere else.

And again.

And again.

And again.

Oftentimes when it does resurface, it does so with more force and intensity.

Have you ever found yourself snapping at the barista at your favorite coffee shop if an order was delayed or incorrect? Maybe losing your mind when someone cuts you off on the highway? Our rational selves know that coffee orders are going to be messed up and that people are going to drive how they drive (more to come on you never know what someone is carrying).

But while our rational selves may know, our emotion can sometimes just spill out as if we can't stop it. When I experience this myself or witness it in others, I know that it's just unhealed pain releasing in other places.

Whack-a-mole.

We have to clean out the "moles" in order to find freedom.

The best way I can explain this is to share an analogy I have used with hundreds of clients. They have all found integrating it into their lives wildly successful.

They have also, however, found that I need to forewarn them to not be eating while I share it.

So, consider this your warning. Put your food down (particularly if you are eating macaroni and cheese or pizza).

We are all familiar with vomiting.

Yes, that awful feeling of when we have a stomach bug or perhaps when we eat something that just isn't settling, and the food makes its way out of our bodies, without our permission. It's just automatic. We can't stop it.

Now, we can all agree that if we ate macaroni and cheese, we would vomit out macaroni and cheese. We would not vomit out pizza, had we eaten macaroni and cheese. That's just not how it works.

Similarly, if what we have pushed down inside of us is anger, we are going to emotionally "spill out" anger.

If it's sadness, that will come out.

In grief, it's a potent combination of some of the nastiest emotional experiences—rage, isolation, loneliness, anger, sadness, blame, judgment, and more.

The truth is that grief not only creates massively intense new emotional experiences, it stirs up what was already inside of us. It churns, twists, taunts, and pulls out emotions and traumas that are buried in the nooks and crannies of our being, most of the time, without any awareness of it.

GLIMMER OF GOLD
Grief can act as a magnifying glass, amplifying any previous hurts, heartaches, and pains you have experienced.

For me, trust, lack of safety, and feeling like I did something wrong (all deep wounds of mine) came flying to the surface. Suddenly, I was crying, apologizing to the cashier if I misread a price, going into a massively intense spout of self-beat up.

It's not logical.

Which is why grief is experienced beyond the mind.

Carrying a Lens

Delayed grief, also known as unresolved or complicated grief, is a type of grief reaction that occurs when the normal process of grieving is prolonged or inhibited. It refers to the experience of grief that doesn't follow the typical pattern of gradually diminishing over time. Instead, the griever may struggle to come to terms with their loss, and the feelings of sadness, pain, and longing persist for an extended period. Or, if they are repressed, they may suddenly come out months, years, or decades later.

However, delayed grief can occur for various reasons, including:

Avoidance: Some individuals may suppress their grief, either consciously or unconsciously, by avoiding thoughts or conversations related to the loss. This can lead to unresolved emotions that resurface later. Or if they do not have supports around them that allow for the processing, they may avoid feeling or discussing their experience.

Multiple Losses: If a person experiences multiple losses in a short period, they might find it challenging to process all the grief at once, leading to delayed grief for some losses.

Unresolved Emotions: Difficult circumstances surrounding the death—such as guilt, anger, or regrets—can hinder the grieving process and cause grief to linger.

Complicated Relationship: The nature of the relationship with the deceased can also impact the grieving process. For example, if the relationship was strained or ambivalent, grief might become more complex.

Lack of Support: A lack of support from family or friends can make it difficult for the bereaved person to express their emotions and work through their grief.

Traumatic Loss: Grief resulting from sudden, unexpected, or traumatic loss can be overwhelming, and the healing process may take longer. The shock and trauma may need to be attended to before healing process can begin.

Permission to Feel

Beyond traditional definitions of delayed grief, I believe there are layers of grief that may be misunderstood as delayed. One of my clients, Sarah, sat on the porch, reflecting on the events of the past year, journaling for our upcoming session. Her heart felt heavy with emotions she thought she had long buried. The pain, the regrets, and the unanswered questions lingered like shadows in the corners of her mind. She didn't understand what was happening. She had gotten a new job—her dream job—and earned a significant raise as well. *This was everything I wanted*, she thought. *What is wrong with me?*

What Sarah was experiencing was despite having a new job in a new company, she was still facing unhealed wounds. Her grief was the grief of the childhood she longed for, grieving a sense of safety in her family and grieving the loss of her voice feeling heard in her family. The truth is, it's never the relationship, the job, the house—all of these things serve as mirrors for what lies within us to heal. And whack-a-mole comes with layers and depths too. We may tend to something at a certain level, but to fully heal, we may be called forward, to go deeper in the same space we already went.

Sarah had feelings of rage, anger, hurt, and betrayal toward her mother. But she never gave herself permission to see her childhood as something to grieve—to feel the grief of not having what she wanted and needed. Now when we grieve these parts of us, we are not doing so to point blame. Sarah's mom did the best she could. Sarah isn't a victim to her childhood, but she was pained by it. There is a massive difference that is often overlooked.

In her childhood, she was punished for speaking up, oftentimes called stupid or laughed at when she shared new ideas or asked questions. Now, over forty years later, after leaving the job she thought was the cause for her unhappiness, she found herself at her dream job, feeling the same exact pain.

She left her workday in tears, feeling, as she wrote, "stupid, embarrassed and like a complete idiot" after a team meeting she had where she felt as though her ideas weren't heard.

The reality is that Sarah was still carrying a lens, one that clouded what she saw and experienced. She was seeing the world through the lens of her pain and traumatic experiences and memories. We are constantly collecting evidence of the stories we tell ourselves. And since Sarah still had to dig deeper to clear that grief of her childhood, she was still collecting evidence to feed the stories that using her voice or sharing ideas would result in pain.

It was clear to her now that healing required more than simply waiting for time to pass. It meant facing the pain head-on, acknowledging the wounds, and offering them the tenderness and compassion they deserved instead of feeling like, "I didn't have it that bad," or, "Other people had it so much worse than me."

When we shame our struggles, it's actually like feeding a growth hormone to our pain and the very things we are seeking reprieve from.

The only way Sarah was going to find freedom was finally allowing herself to feel and express the rage, anger, hurt, sadness, betrayal—the grief she had harbored inside for over thirty years. While she had acknowledged it lightly in our work together, she had resisted fully going to the uncomfortable places of moving and releasing that energy. But she knew it was time.

Sarah learned that her initial judgments of being "messy" were, in fact, judgments that were rooted in fear of being judged herself. In order to get "messy," she had to stop judging herself for doing so.

Strengthening the Scar Tissue

Take a moment to think about how you define happiness and pain.

Is it one or the other?

Do you allow them to coexist?

Write out your vision of happiness. Allow yourself to go to places that seem impossible or unrealistic. Set the timer for eight minutes and just begin writing it out. Don't stop until the timer goes off. When complete, hold on to this for a later chapter where we will explore the power of manifestation combined with tangible action steps. Notice in the meantime what "moles" are popping up that currently stand between you and that vision.

For me, I had to quickly reshape any judgments I had about being messy and allow myself to get out of either/or thinking—that I could either be happy OR grieving. Instead, I shifted into: I can be happy, AND I can be in deep pain from my grief.

It was only from the willingness to redefine my relationship with "happiness" that I could access new levels of it.

And this new relationship did not include forcing or faking smiles to appear happy.

Instead of forcing smiles, I invite you to create a new vision of happiness, alignment, and health.

One that is not tear free.

One that has:

The courage to allow in all waves of this human experience.

The patience to not run from, or fight against, the hard stuff.

The curiosity to process and understand your experience.

The grace and compassion to more deeply connect with yourself as you do.

The strength to truly let things go and bring presence to joy.

The bravery to continue to open up, vulnerably, to love, even when scary.

And to know that layer after layer, you continue to create your very own definition of sheer happiness.

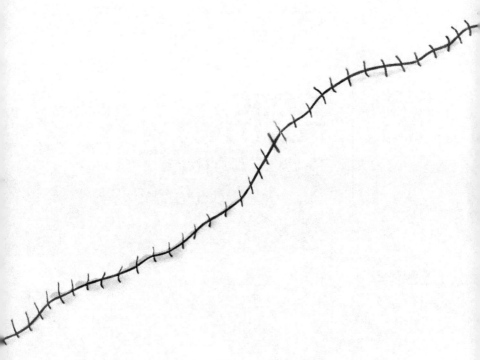

TOXIC
POSITIVITY
STATEMENT
"Good vibes only!"

Release: *Making your vibes or your experience "bad."*

Responses:

Non-Response: Smile and re-direct or end conversation (smiling is optional)

Boundaried Response: That is not only unrealistic, it is not welcome here because it is not my reality.

Educating Response: Truthfully, I do not believe things are "good" or "bad" and that our desire to label them as such is a way of deflecting discomfort and bypassing the truth of our emotional experience. It would support me more to be in conversations around comfortable or uncomfortable "vibes"—and as humans, we face them all. The more we try to stuff down what we perceive as "bad" which is really just uncomfortable, the more we block our actual healing and growth. I know you are on my Team and I value you, so I hope explaining this makes sense and we can align on that moving forward.

Reframe: People seek feelings of predictability and control—which is unrealistic as life and experiences are both unpredictable and most things out of our control. When they say "good vibes only" they are dismissing both the reality and the beauty of the painful, lonely, and dark moments. They are part of the human experience and I choose to see things as comfortable or uncomfortable experiences instead of good or bad.

CHAPTER 11

Grief Is Not a Blank Check:

A HUMBLING AND LIFE-CHANGING LESSON

I can't count the number of times I wanted to scream out loud, "You're upset about THAT! I just lost my child!" or, "Really, you are giving me a hard time; do you have any idea what I have been through?"

But I didn't.

The thoughts would swirl; the temptation would taunt me. But something inside of me knew that doing so was not only overlooking any stories the other person might be carrying, it was, in fact, weaponizing my grief—as if my pain were a blank check to miss deadlines, act however I wanted, and ignore my responsibilities to the world.

The most humbling and life-changing lesson I learned from grief is one that is far from popular.

And while parts of this chapter may shift and shake things, bringing up discomfort like a snow globe being shaken by a small child, I invite you to move through this particular chapter slowly—to reflect, take notes, and take inventory of what comes up in both your body and your mind.

Sometimes slower pacing creates more progress. When we allow things to land, to move through us, and to really settle, we aren't just "checking off the list," we are integrating it into our minds, bodies, and emotions.

Understandably, after I lost Leyden in a case termed a "catastrophe," I carried a lot of pain. I felt like the world had stolen from me, and if there was a God, he MUST be punishing me. Why else would a horror like this be inflicted on me?

I spent day after day after day waking up and staring at pictures, imagining Leyden taking her first steps. *What would her first words be,* I wondered. A thought that kept me up at night was, *What color would her hair be?* Even though she had inherited my big blue eyes, her hair—though light and blondish—had hints of red to it. I found myself imagining not only what color it would be but wondering how long it would be, would it be curly? Would she want to wear it in braids, ponytails, or headbands? When I would see other children playing on the playground, fighting with their siblings, or dancing around the stores, I couldn't keep it together.

So much of my time was focusing on what had been taken from me, I was actually missing the very gifts of what I had been given.

Whatever you believe you can substitute here, but for me, it felt like divine intervention.

I was walking in the streets of Boston, not far from Boston Children's Hospital. This was a walk I had done hundreds of times at this point between Leyden's ninety-nine days in the hospital and my return visits to see friends or attend parent support group meetings.

On this particular day, I was going to see the memorial rocking chair that had been donated in Leyden's name for the eighth floor of the hospital—the floor for babies and children with cardiac complications.

Extra special was that Leyden's cardiologist, in a gesture of love and respect, requested to be part of the assembling of it. Leaving the upper floors of the hospital, where most of his time was spent in white doctor's coats and suits, he would head to the basement with the maintenance department, who was putting the rocker together.

As I approached the hospital, something in me just screamed, "Stop, Melissa!"

Everything went silent around me.

The ambulance sirens, the laughter, horns, buses.

I didn't hear any of them.

I looked up.

The sun was shining directly over the hospital.

Squinting, I held my gaze.

And before I knew it, a thought that had never occurred to me came rushing in, clearer than any other thought I had since Leyden died.

You've been walking around like you were entitled to a healthy child, Me-lissa. But the truth is, we aren't entitled to anything. You can want one, you are worthy of one, but you aren't entitled to anything.

Frozen by this message, unsure how to react, I simply wrote it in my notes app on my phone.

And continued on.

Little by little, I began to slowly move through this concept.

Worthy of everything...

Entitled to nothing...

Was it possible that I had been spending my grief as if I were entitled to something?

Was it possible I had been living my *life* this way?

And I couldn't help but think to myself, *Well, why do I struggle so much with worthiness?* As if I constantly need to prove myself to be worthy.

I began wondering if I had it all backwards.

Entitlement and worthiness.

Not just in my grief but in my life.

I had lived so much of my life thinking that my worthiness depended on external elements: accolades; holding the position of class president or my scholarship for athletics to a D1 school; being in certain relationships.

Had I really spent my entire life outsourcing my worthiness?

And at the same time, was I unknowingly carrying a hidden entitlement that led me to think that things were taken from me and I was a victim to that, instead of being grateful for the very moments and timeline in which I experienced them?

Now, let me be honest, this realization didn't suddenly shift me into being grateful for the nine-month pregnancy and four months of life that I got to experience with Leyden and no longer feeling pain.

But it did open me up to a more expansive, reflective way of thinking.

From that moment, I made a commitment to continually examine where my frustration was coming from and get really clear if it was an unspoken expectation.

A much lighter example would be traffic.

Normally, when stuck in the inevitable traffic Boston is all too well known for, I would find myself frustrated—embarrassingly enough—at times in tears from feeling anxious about where I was supposed to be and how it was all going to be ruined from the damn traffic.

Applying the reflection questions, "Do I have an expectation here that I am not aware of? Is there a level of hidden entitlement?" I could very quickly bring myself to see that I had an expectation that just because I was traveling at a certain time or the news predicted no traffic, I did in fact have an expectation of no traffic.

This level of awareness is one that serves beyond the confines of grief.

Strengthening the Scar Tissue

Reflect on your expectations. Be honest with yourself. Think of these 4 R's and reflect in your journal: Recall, Reveal, Release, Respond. 1—Recall a time you were frustrated. 2—Reveal the real root of that frustration. 3—Release the expectation or entitlement attached to it if applicable. 4—Respond differently next time.

But as I have coached hundreds of clients to understand, awareness is only part of it.

It doesn't actually change behavior.

What we do with awareness is the critical differentiating factor between repeated behavior and growth. Desiring new results, without changing the ways we think and subsequently act, isn't going to create new results. Forcing a new result through "discipline," shame, or stifling our true experience may get a short-term result but certainly not a sustainable one.

GLIMMER OF GOLD
The only way to make long-lasting shifts is to bring a balance of curiosity, compassion, and commitment to choosing alternatively.

A Powerful Trade-In

I developed a four-step method that has helped client after client, through grief and through life, take awareness to action.

When I teach it to my clients, I explain that we are working to trade in "binkies for power tools," meaning that we are letting go of the pacifiers that soothed us and intentionally choosing something more powerful to replace them with.

An easy example I use when helping others integrate this practice in their lives is around Bertucci's rolls.

Picture spending ninety-nine nights in Boston Children's Hospital before the days of Uber Eats or other popular food delivery services.

Between working my job either at the school or from the hospital, (barely) sleeping every night in a fold out chair that turned into a bed, managing Leyden's increasingly intricate health care needs, and round after round with the medical team, food was the last thing on my mind.

While I may have set a record for the number of chicken salad orders I placed from the hospital cafeteria, most nights, by the time I even had a second to think about what I was going to eat for dinner, the cafeteria was closed—which left me with the option of going to the closest restaurant at the time, Bertucci's.

Bertucci's is a popular chain restaurant in New England. Their Italian is well-known, the menu robust, and food very comforting. The only problem is as a gluten-free individual, my options were quite limited. Most times I ordered salmon, salad, or some sort of meat and potatoes options. I never ordered the pizza or pasta, but there was just something about the hug-like feeling the round, infamous Bertucci's rolls provided when they were brought out complimentary to my meal. To be honest, when I was living what felt like complete hell every single day, having a stomachache from a few rolls was the least of my concerns. My diet had been so regimented when Leyden was able to eat to remove anything that might upset my stomach or her stomach—no gluten, dairy, soy, or lactose—because of the "NEC watch" she had been placed on or the possible milk allergy they thought could be at the root of her discomfort. But when Leyden couldn't eat anymore, I didn't care about my own stomachaches.

I cannot count how many conversations, tears, and meals I had at that tiny Bertucci's restaurant. I went with my friends, family, visitors, and even other parents I had met also living in the hospital. In a way, it was like we could breathe. We would sit together after our children were asleep, and the medical rounds complete, and listen to how things were going for one another. We cried, laughed, speculated, asked "what if?" asked "what the f*ck?" and provided space for one another to fully live and express the hell we were all forced to be strong for back in the hospital walls. One of my closest friends at the hospital was another mother whose daughter was just a couple of weeks older than Leyden. Her daughter's diagnosis was more intricate than Leyden's, and many times, I felt guilty because Leyden's case wasn't that bad.

Together, we rode the roller coaster of being a mother to an infant daughter in the cardiac ICU at Boston Children's Hospital. We spent many nights crying over those Bertucci's rolls with no idea how we were going to survive.

When Leyden died, I imagine how scary it must have been for her. I imagine what it would have felt like to watch the room that Leyden had been in, closely located next to her daughter's room, now empty. For us to no longer be there. And to watch another child and family shuffle in to take the highly demanded bed space as if Leyden and I were never there. She was watching the hell I was going through as she was living her own. The fact that she found the courage and strength to come to Leyden's funeral and return to her own sick child is something I still think about with so much admiration and awe.

One Mother's Day after Leyden died, when I was living in downtown Boston, all I was craving were Bertucci's rolls. Before I knew it, I was getting a taxi to take me to Bertucci's right by Boston Children's Hospital. To be honest, it was pretty sad. I sat there crying, so desperately looking for something to help me feel connected to Leyden, to feeling like a mother, to having my baby back. I wish I could go back and hug that version of me, the one looking for anything to feel better. I wish I could tell her that she was going to get through it, to put the rolls down, and to go meet her needs. But I know that was all part of my process. As this wasn't the only time I witnessed a sudden craving for Bertucci's rolls, they had become a linking object for me in my grief. Yet unlike some other linking objects, they weren't serving me, my physical or emotional health, well.

The four-step method I created helped me identify the true need I had and to break myself out of autopilot decisions to get in a taxi and seek comfort in the "binky" of the rolls.

AWARENESS. Step One is bringing awareness to what is transpiring.

CURIOSITY. Step Two is to get curious and compassionate about where this belief, thought, or pattern derives.

REPLACEMENT. Step Three chooses into a replacement to this attachment.

REFLECTION. Step Four is a pause and reflection on how the alternative choice served.

EMOTIONAL REACTION

↓

AWARENESS
What is popping up? What old stories or messages might this be from? What vibe is this? How does this serve me?

↓

CURIOSITY
What am I willing to let go of to create change? Pride/fear/ego/ old stories. Where can I choose to release things that keep me stuck?

↓

REPLACEMENT
What empowering, growth producing energy ca I replace it with? What new habit or narrative will I choose?

↓

REFLECTION
How can I carry this forward? How can I generate momentum and reference this as a new, better serving habit?

↓

INTENTIONAL ACTION

For example, I was aware that I was seeking comfort in something that made me feel closer to the days when my daughter was alive. Then I brought curiosity to where this came from and the pattern of associating a food with being a mom, and having mom conversations, and ending every night with Leyden by my side. Rather than judging myself, I fought the voice saying, "Melissa, that is so pathetic," and loved her harder. I asked her what she needed.

For step three, I integrated a pause. While I had a toolbox of tools, what was missing was the pause I needed before allowing autopilot decision-making to perpetuate a pattern that wasn't actually healing my pain. And then from a place of pause, I leaned on my toolbox to replace the pacifier of the rolls with a power tool. Many times this was calling a friend or doing other things that made me feel like a mom: writing about the lessons I learned from Leyden, going to her memorial tree, working on a charity fundraiser in her honor, and more.

The last step is one that I notice clients (and myself) are tempted to skip, but it must not be skipped because it amplifies the impact and reinforces the benefit (reward signal in our minds) for choosing differently. A day or so later, I spent time reflecting, writing, or voice memo-ing myself on the need that came up and how I chose an empowering way to meet it. I didn't dismiss or make my need wrong. I didn't allow myself to blindly make choices. And when I reinforce this to myself, it creates a positive feeling in choosing differently. It begins to train our minds and brains to do more of what generates the positive feeling.

Strengthening the Scar Tissue

Identify one place in your life where you can transition from a binky to a power tool. Apply the four-step method to it. Use your journal to help you work through the steps. Like anything, the four-step method takes time and patience. In the beginning, it may feel laborious, as it is interrupting what has brought comfort. Commitment and consistency to integrating it allows it to not only get results but to become a very natural trajectory your thoughts, words, and actions go. And ultimately, it is a practice in taking new levels of responsibility for our healing. Common binkies can include alcohol, substance usage, binging on TV or Netflix, food, sex, and even seemingly healthy choices like exercise. While it is tempting to reach for the things that feel good in the moment, to rely on a partner or friend to do our healing for us, or ask for everyone in our lives, jobs, and passersby to treat us differently because of what we are carrying, we get to remember that can actually be a way of weaponizing grief—not only weaponizing it externally, but most importantly, weaponizing it internally.

When we are not aware, our grief can be something we use to beat ourselves up over and over, as if we are our own punching bag. With awareness,
tools, and consistency, we can move to a more empowering, intentional, and
loving space for ourselves and everyone else in our lives. Grief weaves an intricate and unavoidable thread, touching us all at some point in our journey. It is
an emotion that knows no boundaries, transcending culture, age, and circumstance. While grief is an ever-present companion, each individual's experience
of it as unique as our own DNA.

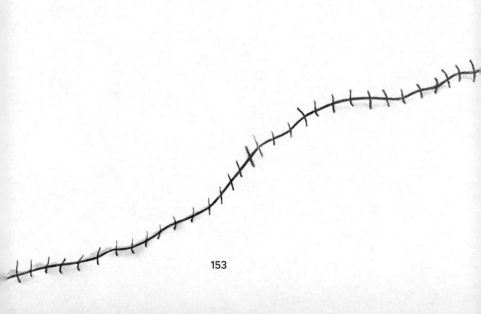

TOXIC POSITIVITY STATEMENT

"You'll get over it..."

Release: *Dismissing the reality of pain experienced right now, feeling unseen.*

Responses:

Non-Response: Smile and re-direct or end conversation (smiling is optional)

Boundaried Response: I'll get through it—not over it—but that's not exactly a helpful response.

Alternative: Maybe that's how you were supported or what you tell yourself, but that is not supportive for me.

Educating Response: I know you don't mean to be hurtful, but the truth is that hurts me and makes me not want to be close to you or communicate with you on what I am going through. If you don't want me to come to you with my challenges, I respect that. But hearing "you'll get over it" just makes me feel like I am an inconvenience to you or that I shouldn't feel what I am genuinely feeling right now.

Reframe: People do not know how to handle difficult things and subconsciously their human nature has them wanting to rush through, minimize, or avoid them.

CHAPTER 12

A Crowded Loneliness:

GRIEF HIDDEN BENEATH THE SURFACE

The cart felt as though it were filled with concrete blocks. I slowly pushed it down the aisle of Trader Joe's as if it were a football sled. I was using my entire body to move in a strength training session. Lights shone so bright as if they were blinding me, and while there was music playing overhead, I couldn't hear it. It was all a blur.

How are all these people just living their lives like nothing happened? I thought. *Don't they know that Leyden died?* Tears welled in my eyes as I tried to pick one leg up, then the other, and move through the store.

It had taken a lot for me to make it to a crowded, public place for the first time, wearing my wrinkled clothing I had picked up from the floor of my bedroom. Unplanned, it had become my summer uniform, each day dropping them to the ground and the next day picking them back up again—the same outfit, but my shorts were falling off my waist. Eating was nearly impossible.

If it weren't for the, "Excuse meeeeee," and "What are you doing?" before finally I heard, "MOVE!" I don't know when I would have realized that I was standing in the middle of the store, frozen, trying to remember what I came to the store for, unable to say a word out loud as if my throat and mouth were paralyzed, and each word was a heavy weight I just couldn't lift.

I looked around, realizing I was in the middle of Trader Joe's on a busy Saturday and blocking people from quickly moving through the aisle.

I don't know how many people commented at me. But the last one that I heard, when I looked up at the woman, I wanted so badly to explain, apologize, and move along. And I couldn't. Tears moved from filling my eyes to streaming down my face. I left my cart and left the store, got into my car, and started sobbing.

After a few minutes, I caught my breath, and in silence, I drove home.

I would imagine if anyone in that grocery store knew my daughter had just died, I would have been supported. They likely would have treated me compassionately, patiently, lovingly.

To this day, people still treat me differently when they find out I am a bereaved mother.

At first glance, they see a blonde-haired, blue-eyed millennial.

Why do we consider someone more worthy of love once we learn that they are hurting? Or healing?

Days later, I was in the passenger seat driving down the overcrowded streets of Boston. Storrow Drive is this mini highway between the busy streets of downtown and the Charles River that defines so much of Boston's geography. Well-known for traffic, it wasn't a surprise that we had found ourselves in stop-and-go. Out of nowhere, a black car darting between lanes, trying to get one car ahead of another, cut us off.

My friend had some words for the driver.

I stared ahead and whispered, "What if they just lost their child?"

After Trader Joe's, this became one of my default responses.

"What if they just lost their child?"

While it's possible that they just lost their child, this phrase represents a recognition, an acknowledgement that everyone is carrying a story.

Grief is a universal experience.

Maybe the driver of the black car didn't just lose a child.

But maybe they did.

Or perhaps they are on their way to the hospital where a sick loved one awaits.

Maybe they just lost their job, are navigating a divorce, feel lost in this world from losing their own identity, a pet, or feeling completely powerless because they and their partner are unable to have a child.

GLIMMER OF GOLD

While grief can feel like the most lonely experience, the truth is, it's one of the most widely shared experiences.

The Power of a Question

There are two components here that are extremely important to understand when navigating our journeys of life and grief.

1. Grief is a universal truth. Rather than pretend it doesn't exist, avoid it, or hide from it, how can we create the space and tools to actively move through it?

2. Grief is something we all experience at one time or another in our lives.

An activity that I have used with hundreds of my clients is, "What else could be true?"

During one of our sessions, Tara—a forty-four-year-old woman, married, and a very successful working professional—came to me exhausted. Her pet had just died, and in addition to losing her dog, it triggered challenges she had with infertility and choosing a family dynamic that was without children.

She said, "I don't know how I can keep going."

We began to unpack the heaviness. Not only was she grieving the loss of her pet, but it triggered unresolved grief around her infertility and feelings of shame, sadness, and self-judgment that came with this experience for her. Tara was experiencing hyper-vigilance and felt very on edge. She was reading into things such as an email, text message, comment made at work, and even went as far as when she saw her husband on his phone, creating stories in her head that he must be talking with another woman. All of this led to her snapping, being impatient, and incredibly sensitive and fearful of what was going to go wrong next. Of course Tara was exhausted.

Through our work together, we not only integrated nervous system regulation tools, which we will explore in the next chapter, but we worked on strengthening her emotional agility. Her husband on his phone, the emails and texts she referenced as stressful things for her, were stressful because of the emotional responses and thoughts that were applied automatically without realizing it.

When we used the strategy of, "What else could be true?" I coached her to come up with five other possibilities. I told her that I didn't care how insane the possibilities were, the point was to train her brain to get out of tunnel vision, and focusing on her fears and unhealed pain, to expand and create a sense of safety in looking at other possibilities.

For example, with the email that asked to set up a meeting that resulted in Tara feeling anxious that something was wrong or she was in trouble, we looked at what else could be true. Maybe she was getting a raise, perhaps the person was quitting, maybe they had a new idea they wanted to run by her, or wanted her feedback on something else happening. And just for the sake of teaching her brain to dream big, we laughed and said maybe the company is paying for everyone to travel to Hawaii for a week! It turned out that the company was afraid of losing Tara and wanted to talk with her about how they could keep her and what she needed. She did get a raise.

With her husband, when we used, "What else could be true," Tara said he could be texting with a family member, scrolling on social media, reading an article online, watching videos on YouTube, and in dreaming big, we said he could be shopping for an amazing gift or travel opportunity for her. When she allowed herself to see there are many options outside of the story her mind was creating, she was able to calmly and productively articulate her curiosity for what he was so focused on in his phone without judging, snapping, or assuming. And, she laughed when he shared that he had discovered a new word game that he was loving playing. This strengthened their bond and connection, and she was also able to ask for time where he was more present, which he provided. He also was able in this conversation to speak about how he had noticed her grief and anxiety and wasn't sure what to do, and probably was playing the game more often in these moments, as he was nervous himself. From building emotional agility through the firing thought patterns and pain flying in her grief, they had a conversation that cultivated more connection and brought them closer to one another.

"What else could be true?" is a simple method you can use to open up to other possibilities than the fear that grief often drives within the narratives running internally.

When we practice doing this internally, we can do it more widely too.

Another really simple way to integrate this is to look at the tone of voice we assign to a text message or an email. I always find it fascinating when I hear someone read an email back to me, assigning the tone of voice to it that they (subconsciously) attached.

The text, "Call me," could have many tones assigned—each of which creates a wildly different experience.

An email saying, "I'd like to discuss this more," could also have many tones assigned, each with different meanings.

Strengthening the Scar Tissue

Practice asking yourself "What else could be true?" when feeling upset or frustrated with others. Release judgment around words, written and spoken, and become aware when you assign meanings or tones to texts, emails, social posts.

Another great way to practice emotional agility, staying present, not making assumptions, and not exhausting yourself with your own assigned tones or stories is to practice reading an email or text in multiple tones of voice. Doing so will actually train your brain to begin to stay open to diverse ways people can communicate and respond.

You Know What They Say About Assumptions...

When I left Trader Joe's that day in tears, there was a phrase I kept saying to myself and clung to dearly:

"Don't take anything personally."

This is one of the Four Agreements from the book, *The Four Agreements*, written by Don Miguel Ruiz, and draws on wisdom from Toltec beliefs and practices. I discovered the book when Tom Brady, the then quarterback of the New England Patriots, shared in a press conference that he read it before each season to help himself mentally prepare for the roller coaster that each season brought. In my desperation of my grief journey to prepare myself for my own roller coaster, I consumed the book in a day—and reread it multiple times.

I'll never forget hearing things in attempts to provide comfort such as, "At least she wasn't older..." implying that my pain would be worse if Leyden had lived to be older. Or, "You should really read *Man's Search for Meaning*, a book about a survivor of the Holocaust; it will really bring you perspective." Had I not worked on my own energy, the concept of not taking things personally, I would have likely responded very differently than I did in those moments. But I was able to see that the human speaking to me was just trying to say, "I love you; you'll be okay, and I don't know what to say, but I really want to say something to help." Or in the case of keeping the baby alive, was just so entangled in their journey as a new parent, they weren't aware of the piercing pain of those words for a mother who couldn't keep her baby alive.

Not taking anything personally is one of the most accelerating tools to find freedom in your life and in your grief. Beyond not taking it personally from others, I learned to not take it personally from the Universe/Source/God, (insert whatever you may believe in). I'll never forget, with tears rolling down my cheeks, asking a mentor at my church, "Am I being punished for mistakes that I have made in my life or things I did wrong?"

She responded by saying, "I don't know about your God, but I like to believe my God would never punish me, and especially not through the loss of the life of my child," which reminded me that I was looking for ways to make this about me. But truly, it was not.

You will be met time and time again in your healing journey with unsolicited advice, words meant to heal but might hurt. You will lose friendships or feel distance in them. You will see things on social media or in the news that trigger you. This is the reality. Grief is like walking through a minefield where you have no idea when a trigger might go off at any given moment. When we alleviate the layers of taking things personally and remember nothing actually is in fact, personal, we empty so much heaviness that is carried.

Though it sounds simple, it is not easy.

Not taking it personally doesn't mean that we don't need to put boundaries in place.

We can not take something personally, which alleviates emotional drain.

AND we can put boundaries in place too.

When Tara talked with her husband about his phone usage, she made a request for a boundary to be around how much time was spent on the phone. Boundaries can be one of the most loving forms of self-care and also strengthen relationships. Remember that no one is a mind reader. When we responsibly communicate our needs and what is or isn't okay with us, we create clear expectations and a sense of safety with multiple people knowing what is and what isn't okay. Not having to guess if someone is withholding their discomfort or dissatisfaction saves an incredible amount of emotional energy.

Strengthening the Scar Tissue

Think of something right now that is taking your attention or energy, something that you may be worried about—a text you received, something you observed, or maybe an email. Write out five possibilities around "what else could be true." Make sure one of the possibilities is so wildly unlikely, and trust that in doing so, you are training your brain to stay open to many possibilities. From openness to unexpected magic, we actually can create and invite in unexpected magic.

The version of me that didn't understand how everyone was carrying on in the world like nothing happened was humbled, deeply, by grief. Grief held a magnifying glass to the truth that no one else's life was about me. The world was not about me. The masses of people and the world would go on without Leyden. When I learned not to take this personally, I eliminated unnecessary layers of heaviness and was able to more acutely focus on my own pain and grief from my loss.

TOXIC POSITIVITY STATEMENT

"Focus on the positive, not the negative..."

Release: *The need to make a choice and the pressure to not feel the feels.*

Responses:

Non-Response: Smile and re-direct or end conversation (smiling is optional)

Boundaried Response: Please don't tell me where I need to focus my energy—that's my decision.

Educating Response: Do you know that when people do that, they end up bottling things up and that leads to physical, mental, and emotional health issues. They don't actually heal from what they are going through and if we don't heal what hurt us we end up hurting other people or ourselves. So I understand that the negative—or challenging—things happening are not pleasant to talk about but I am committed to working through them and not avoiding. If you want to support me, I would need you to align with that. And I acknowledge that isn't easy and understand if you can't do that.

Reframe: I don't expect everyone to get it or have the tools to support me in the challenging parts of my journey. I honor my own experience and allow the true healing to come from a growth mindset that looks ahead and finds the opportunities while also a compassion and nurturing for the pain and hurt I am experiencing.

PART FOUR

THE
REBULDING

I didn't know it was *possible*
to hold both—unrelenting *grief*
and genuine *joy*——but I learned.
I learned that *healing* doesn't
mean you're done *hurting*. It
means you've built the capacity to
carry both.

CHAPTER **13**

Threads of Gold:

ALLOWING YOUR HEART TO BREAK AGAIN AND AGAIN

I stared at my computer screen through tears; the words were impossible to find and even harder to arrange. My gaze drifted to the sweet prints and soft blankets that danced between the bouncer, Pack 'n Play, and crates of books, each book with a handwritten note in it:

Dear baby, we give you hugs and kisses through your mom's belly every day! We can't wait to give you hugs, and we think hugs with two hands are the best. We wonder what kind of hugs you will like?

Dear baby, the doctor says you are very active! Mommy does a special yoga class for moms with babies in their belly—so you are already a yogi! We wonder what you will enjoy when you grow up! All our love, Mom and Dad.

The crib, carefully chosen after hours of debating which color, size, and style was "right" now looked so "wrong" as it sat empty. Fantasies of my daughter Leyden's dedication ceremony (my church's version of the more traditional baptism) had been replaced by the nightmare of planning her funeral.

How can I possibly find the words to capture her life? And...how can I possibly survive her death?

As I sat trying to type, it felt as though I were an empty body going through the motions—almost as if I could see the parts of me shattered all around the floor. I envisioned myself as the lamp sitting on my end table that had fallen off the ledge into a million little pieces on the floor, unrecognizable. As I envisioned this, I decided, no, I hadn't been knocked off a shelf; someone (the Universe, Source, God, whatever you believe—at this time I was struggling to believe in anything) had taken a hammer or mallet like the ones you see at carnivals where people lift them over their heads and bang them as heavily as they can to measure their strength. But instead of doing so to win a giant stuffed teddy bear, this had happened to me, my life, myself. And it wasn't a game.

I searched for inspirational quotes and poems on the internet.

Nothing seemed to quite capture the feeling of having my child die in my arms.

A phrase I couldn't let go of was how her case was termed "a catastrophe."

There was nothing I could do to fix that, but it certainly drove a deep desire for my words, the message I shared at Leyden's funeral, to be perfect.

Perfect. That word swirled around in my head. *I have to be perfect.* Perfect was the word that held catastrophe at bay in my mind, pushed it right back out the door it waltzed in from. But only momentarily. As I strived for perfection, catastrophe slipped between the cracks, seeping through every opening possible.

I scrolled online for hours for the perfect urn, for the perfect flowers, the perfect invitations, the perfect quotes for my speeches. My outfit that day needed to be perfect as well, my dress couldn't have a crease, and my hair needed to sit frizz-free on my shoulders. *I needed to be perfect.* It was odd how quickly I became obsessed with perfection, something that had never bothered me before. But after Leyden's case had been called a catastrophe, I felt this pressure. I had failed, so I better not create another catastrophe again. I have to be perfect.

Tears poured down my face with frustration and fear.

I have already messed up her life, I thought, I cannot mess up how I manage her death.

As someone who fills my social media, office, and home with inspirational quotes, there must be something I can find that makes sense, I thought.

I remembered the words I spoke at my high school graduation. As the class president giving a speech to my peers, I said, "Don't cry because it's over, smile because it happened."

Seventeen-year-old me had no idea the depths of pain that came with "endings."

I thought packing up and going to live forty-five minutes away at college, no longer spending my Friday nights watching football games on the sidelines wearing my then-boyfriend's jersey, was a loss.

I urged my classmates to celebrate what we experienced instead of feeling the sadness of the conclusion of it all. And really, I was reinforcing this message for myself.

That seventeen-year-old version of me had no idea what she was in for.

I Googled for what felt like hours, envisioning the million pieces of my heart and soul on the floor around me. I finally input the words "life shattered" and "re-piecing yourself together."

And somehow I landed on articles around a concept I had never heard of: kintsugi. I suddenly felt seen.

Mending with Gold

I earnestly read about the history of lacquerware in Asia. Truthfully, it was a nice distraction from the heaviness of my grief. I learned how these works of art, both functional and beautiful, are largely associated with Asian culture. While the history of creating such works of art is ancient, the manner in which broken or shattered masterpieces are handled is relatively new. In the fifteenth century, a Japanese military director was devastated when his prized tea bowl broke. He sent it for repair and when it returned, the cracks of the gorgeous tea bowl were mended with large, unsightly, metal staples. Dissatisfied, he directed his craftsmen to find a more aesthetically pleasing way of fixing the bowl. This launched a quest among the men, and it wasn't long before they were mixing gold, silver, and platinum dust into each repair. This mending practice known as kintsugi literally translates to "golden joinery." Kintsugi was so popular that craftsmen were accused of smashing and breaking pottery so that they could then repair it more beautifully. This changed the way in which broken and damaged masterpieces were viewed. Cracks became an illuminated and celebrated part of the object.

It dawned on me that I was on my own search, desperately trying to find a repair—except I had no interest in highlighting or celebrating my damages nor did I want gold dust to fill my cracks. I wanted to find emotional superglue and put the thousands of pieces of me perfectly back in place. I wanted things to go back to the way they were.

But what do we do when we desperately want something back that has absolutely no chance of coming back?

Philosophically, the practice of kintsugi draws on the Buddhist concept that there is beauty in imperfection. Breaks and tears represent a crucial and defining moment in the object's history. I reflected on how while none of us get to choose whether or not we will encounter hardships, each of us can design how we face them.

Allowing Two Things to Be True

Time doesn't heal. Time simply gives us the opportunity to choose into healing. Trauma and growth can coexist. It is not "either/or." I learned the importance of replacing the word "or" with "and." Two things can be true at the same time. For example, I can be happy OR I can be grieving. Replacing "or" with "and" offers an opportunity for happiness and grief, trauma and growth, joy and pain to coexist. I didn't have to choose. And neither do you. Being real with ourselves creates space for this.

We don't need to feel good all the time. And we don't need to feel "good" OR "bad." We can feel pain and gratitude, love and loss, all simultaneously. Replace the word "or" with "and" to create more space for differing emotional experiences.

There is an element of radical responsibility in grief. This is hard when grief naturally lends itself to a victim or pained energy. I was fully in my right to be a victim to my daughter's case, which was termed a catastrophe. But not choosing that, and rather to take massive ownership for my healing, changed my life.

Not everyone will get it, and that's OK. Let go of the expectation of people to show up in a certain way, respond a certain way, or support a certain way. When we truly release expectations like this, it's freeing. Understand how each person contributes, or does not, to your path forward, and instead of making anyone wrong, focus energy on what continues to propel you.

Strengthening the Scar Tissue

Find opportunities to replace "or" with "and." And allow yourself the space and time for these feelings to coexist, not in competition with each other, but rather simultaneously.

Labels and Our Identities

In order for me to rebuild myself, I needed to look at how I identified myself. *New York Times* bestselling author Sharon Salzberg wrote, "There is no controlling the unfolding of life." In order for me to survive the pain and loss, I needed to harness my desire to fight it. In fact, I had to surrender to it. Surrender to the fact that yes, I was shattered. Surrender to the fact that no, Leyden wasn't coming back. And surrender to the truth that there was no way things would ever feel normal or the way they "should be" again.

I preface this with an important side note that, as I am sure you would as well, I would trade this opportunity, at any moment, to have my daughter, Leyden, back. But, like most adversities we have all encountered, the option to choose isn't offered. So, when we face such powerless situations, what choice do we have?

Losing Leyden came with the loss of my identity. From the moment Leyden came into this world, I embraced my instinctual maternal nature. I even bought maternity clothes long before I needed to wear them, just because I wanted to dress the part. I'll never forget being at my friend's cookout, not showing whatsoever, and changing into a maternity one-piece that was way too large on me because I was so excited to step into my role as Mama.

Strengthening the Scar Tissue

Take a moment to think about the identities and labels that you have lost in the grief you are carrying.
Honor them.
Love your connection to them.
Acknowledge that in order to heal, we must find the courage to thank them for the purpose they served and release them.

As we dig deeply into finding our new identities, we realize that every identity or role we play, every relationship dynamic, and every job or position we hold is simply a hat, a costume that we put on and take off. Sometimes we don't take it off until we are forced to.

None of these "costumes" are in fact our true selves, our true identity.

And when we are standing there naked, in the mirror, our costumes ripped out of our hands, it can be wildly scary to sit and look at ourselves and wonder, "Who am I now?"

We may want to sprint to find another costume, something to adorn to provide a sense of belonging, a sense of purpose, or a sense of self.

Grief begs us to stand in front of the mirror and look at the stripped-down versions of us.

And when we try to run, grief walks us back to that mirror with a firm hand on our back, a gentle hand on our chin, lifting our gaze to see ourselves, fully, and connect deeply with the soul staring back.

GLIMMER OF GOLD
The grief of who you once were and reconciliation with who you continue to be needs to be tended to in order to reintegrate and heal.

As we rebuild ourselves, we have the (unwelcome) opportunity to build our identity around nothing but who we are—something we aren't taught in traditional society programming. We are taught that our identity is in our family, in the work we do, accolades we have, number of followers on social media, money in our bank account, cars in our driveway, titles we carry, degrees or certifications we carry, children we parent, parents we care for... Those define our identity.

One of my clients who served in the military now focuses his work on helping other veterans recover from the loss, pain, and trauma experienced. Exiting the military, he explained, is losing the identity that you came to know for yourself. He shared how when everything was so intensely wrapped around a collective mission, a uniform, structure, routine, and a purpose outside of oneself, when leaving, it is common that those who served feel a sense of disconnection from who they are, as if their identity remained in the military, but their life continued outside of it. The grief of who they once were and reconciliation with who they continue to be needs to be tended to in order to reintegrate and heal.

As relentless and exhausting as grief is, grief asks us to see ourselves beyond all the things that can be taken from us at any moment.

To see ourselves for the masterpiece that we are at our core, without anything else.

To love that version of us.

And to know when we connect to it at the deepest level, our identity can never be lost, because our identity lies within us.

A Stronger and Deeper Worthiness

As someone who chronically sought external validation and acceptance to feel worthy, this was a wildly hard lesson for me to learn. And one I continually practice.

Grieve the old version of you.

Grieve the people who don't relate to new versions of you.

Create new identities.

But connect to your truest identity—identity of self.

Chip and Joanna Gaines captivated the world with their show *Fixer Upper*. Their storyline is basic: a talented couple takes the worst houses and transforms them into dream homes. But their process is unique. During "Demo Day" on the show, the construction team tears apart wall after wall, pulls out windows, and rips off siding. What distinguishes Chip and Joanna is that this becomes a treasure hunt as they search the demolition to uncover hidden gems—things that can only be discovered when the home is destroyed. Once-disguised elements are uniquely showcased in the finished product, hidden treasures of the past uncovered as celebrations of distinct character.

Strengthening the Scar Tissue

When we strip away all the sense of identity that is external or out of our control, we actually strengthen our truest identity—our connection to ourselves in the soul. I invite you to join me to reflect upon the unspoken opportunities that destruction, adversity, and loss provide for us to reconstruct our worlds with mindfulness, beauty, and choice.

An Invisible String

It had been hours of searching on Google for the "perfect" poem to share at Leyden's funeral—finding myself in black holes of reading about lacquerware in Asia, thinking about TV shows I had watched, and looking for any inspiration or magical light bulb to help me get clear in what to say to truly honor my daughter.

But instead I just felt haunted, I had messed everything up. I told myself this every night while I lay awake. I could feel the guilt and grief cloaked in the darkness of the night, lurking under my bed or around the door frame of my bedroom. They were waiting for me to slip up again so they could consume me. My identity felt as if it now belonged to those shadows that stalked my halls at night.

While I needed to redefine my identity as Leyden's mom, I was still her mother. And speaking about her life was my privilege and responsibility that I didn't want to mess up.

My eyes returned to the books with the handwritten notes:

Dear baby, your mom and dad love you so much already. We have family all over the country. No matter where we are, or what we are doing, we believe an invisible string of love keeps us all connected. Always. Hugs and kisses, Mom and Dad.

I observed how my own words, written to Leyden before she entered this world, had a whole new meaning now that she had left it. An invisible string would keep us connected.

Strangely, I felt a sense of hope—that maybe love itself was my superglue, my gold. Maybe filling my cracks and piecing back the parts of me that were all over the floor would start with love and grow with an acceptance of the new ways in which love would be expressed. Grief is really just love that lost its home. And I was going to have to learn how to build a new home for this love to live in.

Closing my eyes, I realized that there were no words on Google I was going to find.

There was no new identity as a mother.

I had been writing to my daughter before I met her, so I was going to write to her after I lost her.

Suddenly, the words poured out—a final letter to my daughter expressing the love that had no baby to hold, one that her uncle would read at her memorial ceremony:

You came into this world, with a gentle and kind soul,
And a heart that gave love freely, despite its challenging holes.
Your loving big blue eyes, talked to us each day,
Showing us your wonder, you had so much to say.
You taught your mom and dad a lot,
With your bravery and your might.
Face fear, keep perspective, share love,
You reminded us through your fight.
The most powerful lesson you taught us,
That selfless true love holds.
A lesson you challenged your parents to learn,
When you needed us to let you go.
Leyden, we love you.
You are the perfect gift.
We miss your smell, your touch, your smile.
We miss your scoochy face.

We hope you feel our pride, our love,
As you rest in your new place.

Maybe remembering as we rebuild ourselves that love, for ourselves, and a remembrance that love can never be destroyed, it can only be transformed, is actually our superglue, our gold. And as we re-piece ourselves, rebuilding one moment and breath at a time, we may find strength in knowing we will never be the same masterpieces as we once were or wanted to be, but we can still be a masterpiece. And perhaps, just perhaps, we can be an even more beautiful version of what we once were.

TOXIC POSITIVITY STATEMENT

"Don't be dramatic..."

Release: *Shame for having a human experience.*

Responses:

Non-Response: Smile and re-direct or end conversation (smiling is optional)

Boundaried Response: If you think this is an expression of drama, you aren't the person I can talk to about what is going on.

Educating Response: I am curious to know what you think is dramatic about this? I ask because this is very real for me and you are important to me. I want to be able to connect with you and be close in the fire of this pain and heartache, but I don't want to be told I am being dramatic.

Reframe: People will project their own unhealed wounds or experiences onto me and I have no control over that. If I am perceived as dramatic by someone it does not mean that is my truth. I get to honor the depth of my emotions in ways that are supportive, healthy and expressing.

CHAPTER 14

The Freedom:

SURRENDERING TO YOUR GRIEF

Fight-or-flight is real.

And so is my innate default to fight like hell.

I've historically done this so intensely that "Meli-Melichick" (in reference to the New England Patriots' head football coach, Bill Belichick) became my nickname because I would predictably break down any challenge faced into tiny little pieces to understand, master, and conquer.

I wouldn't stop until I studied and figured out how to master something.

I am sure that several of my former partners found this to be exhausting.

I found it to be effective.

When I was told I could possibly play Division Three field hockey in college, I worked relentlessly until I landed myself a scholarship to play at the Division One level and eventually captain the team.

The cubicle job that wasn't fulfilling to me? I jumped without a parachute and learned as I figured out how to piece together multiple jobs while building a new career. And I even ended up earning a higher salary than I did at that cushy corporate job.

The dream job that I applied for and didn't get? I dedicated the next year to preparing and practicing, which worked favorably because I beat out over three hundred other applicants to get the job at an even bigger district that paid more. I was the youngest female in my role in the state, and I knew this was another way my grit and grind paid off.

So naturally when grief, my most massive, monstrous, and painful opponent presented itself, I was ready to fight. I would tear it down into tiny pieces, study it, master it, and then conquer it.

You want to smash my heart? I thought. Bring it on, grief. You are going down.

I joined every bereaved parent group that I could, hired a grief coach, and signed up to run a marathon in Leyden's honor for the very hospital where she took her last breath. I studied grief, read book after book, sought out podcasts and TED talks, and I even traveled outside of the country by myself to hear a world renowned grief speaker.

I now envision grief watching me run in circles with my boxing gloves on, smiling knowingly, seeing my desperation to escape the pain and to "beat it." I threw punch after punch. And it wasn't until I was curled up in a ball, face stained with tears, unable to fight anymore, that I realized *there is no beating grief.*

And in trying to resist and fight my opponent, I was utterly exhausting myself.

Grief is patient.

Grief is stubborn.

Grief is demanding.

It demands to be tended to in a way that is not fighting it nor fleeing from it—which is really hard when as humans, we are wired to do one of the two when pain presents. It is also expansive.

We are All Grieving Something

Grief is too commonly dismissed as solely related to death.

But it's much more powerful than that.

So rather than run from grief, avoid talking about it, or fight it, if we know that the energy of grief will present many times throughout our life, and in truth, can exist daily on a micro level when we are not going through macro level experiences, how can we best equip ourselves to take on our opponent without exhausting ourselves?

The energies and experiences of grief apply so widely and understanding this is critical to being able to truly move through whatever challenge you are currently facing or for the future ones that inevitably await.

In a world of little certainty and few universals, grief is one that we all collectively will experience, multiple times, in our lives. We don't always know when, where, or how. We just know that we will encounter this unwelcome opponent.

Whatever your grief is, I am so sorry.

It may show up as feeling no hope for the future, an ache in your gut that nothing can soothe. Maybe you are just numb...

Whatever you are feeling I am telling you right now, you have the right to mourn the way you need to. There is one thing I will always stand by, and that is the need to authentically grieve. So right now I am asking you to listen to that feeling deep down that says to scream at the top of your lungs, that is telling you to write, paint, workout. Whatever it may be, let the energy move through you, in your own way. Answer those callings with reverence. Authentic grieving doesn't give you the right to be an asshole, but it tells you there simply is no one way to go about and to honor who you are in your grief.

If you haven't checked any of the boxes we have explored so far, it's possible you are still experiencing grief.

Chosen grief is when we actively choose a loss in our lives. This doesn't mean that we choose to take someone off of life support. These losses are massively prevalent, widely misunderstood, and commonly dismissed because it was a "choice."

Ending a relationship that you cared deeply for but is no longer serving you is chosen grief.

Moving out of a community that you love and were rooted in, is chosen grief.

Leaving a job or career, and not only that lifestyle but that identity, is chosen grief.

I found myself sobbing for both Meghan and Prince Harry when watching the Netflix series *Harry & Meghan*. To be honest, as someone who avoids much of the mainstream news, I had not heard of the happenings that transpired within the British royal family.

In the series, I witnessed them experiencing what most people will never acknowledge as grief: chosen grief.

In chosen grief, society often dismisses the heartaches, losses, and pain that accompanies it, because it was a choice.

While it is certainly different from other types of grief we have explored, chosen grief needs a seat at the table.

The stifling of our grief because we feel as though we are not entitled to, or worthy of, truly grieving the losses we are enduring amplifies the pain that we feel while simultaneously denying us the very supports that are considered acceptable when grief is *not chosen*.

As discussed, grief includes losing the future you envisioned, your family dynamic, home, friendships, and relationships, damaged reputation, and sense of safety and stability in the world.

The energy of grief doesn't change because it has been chosen.

In fact, I believe that opting into heartbreak and suffering requires a level of courage that is unique to this particular type of grief.

Strengthening the Scar Tissue

Take a moment to reflect on difficult decisions you have made to leave something that is no longer serving you and your life.
Look at the costs that you paid in many ways.
Can you, in this moment, give yourself permission to grieve these losses?
To feel the pain?
To feel the fear?
To feel the instability?
Now consider people around you who may have opted into their own forms of chosen grief.
Can you support them in giving themselves permission to grieve those losses too?
Taking this a step forward, can you celebrate the courage and trust it takes to believe that putting ourselves through pain is worth our greatest evolution and good?

When I look at some of the greatest change agents of our world, so many of them were willing to give up a sense of self, safety in the world, a feeling of being understood, liked, popular—they were willing to step into spaces of loneliness, judgment, isolation, and more.

Because they believed doing so was in the interest of not only themselves but of our society.

Making such decisions is incredibly painful. We must not deny ourselves the space to grieve the subsequent experiences that come with these decisions.

Leaving a partnership with the person I thought I was going to marry was one of the most difficult decisions I have made in my entire life, if not the most difficult.

Losing my daughter Leyden came with no choice.

Stepping into the energy and experiences of grief again, through my own choosing, was no easy feat.

In fact, the healing work I needed to do was very similar.

I needed to grieve.

There were days I spent in bed, crying for hours on end. Calling on my Teammates and leveraging the exact tools I learned through the loss of Leyden got me through.

Had I not given myself permission to grieve, I would never have healed.

Giving ourselves permission to grieve is a critical step in the healing process.

Truthfully, I experienced so many people in my world not giving themselves permission to grieve, even when they had no choice.

Chosen or not, grief is an energetic force that cannot be stuffed down. It cannot be shamed, dismissed, or placed in a hierarchy of worthiness to be tended to. While there are different depths of grief, intensities of it, of course, they all demand our attention and healing.

Without doing so, we are not only playing whack-a-mole, we are feeding the moles steroids that will amplify them until they become so big, so painful, and so suffocated in the tiny space we have tried to keep them in that they erupt.

GLIMMER OF GOLD
The peace is on the other side of the burn.

Permission to Grieve

A common theme I have found in my work is when people feel permission to grieve, they feel relief. One of my clients was struggling as his mother was ill with Alzheimer's disease. Her lack of memory was painful, and each day he spoke with her, he was grieving the relationship that they had. Yet she was still alive, so he had not recognized that he was grieving. I explained to him that he was navigating anticipatory grief as well as the grief of what was—in the relationship with his mother, the conversations they had shared, and the woman he knew her to be. I said that it was like going up a roller coaster, the knots and fear that creep in as you feel yourself going higher and higher, awaiting the drop. But unlike a roller coaster, he hadn't chosen to be on this, he didn't know when it was going to "drop," and it was going to be a lot more than a few minutes of feeling like he wanted to vomit.

Please know that your grief is real. We do not want to add heaviness by thinking the pain you are feeling is unwarranted as a loss hasn't transpired. Your grief is real.

Grief is cold, lonely, and isolating.

It challenges your sense of safety and leaves you with a "shaky" feeling of distrust.

Sometimes we compensate by seeking ways to feel trust and safety. This is why therapists and counselors will urge you to be cautious of major decisions made and relationships entered when in such a vulnerable state.

I remember the weeks and months after losing Leyden when I wanted to move, adopt a child, and get pregnant all at the same time, my grief coach patiently smiling and saying, "Let's wait to make any decisions, okay?"

Other times in grief, we build walls to prevent ourselves from being hurt. This is why therapists and counselors will urge you to stay connected with other people, to "schedule in" grief time, and to be sure to leave the house.

For me, leaving the house was hard. I felt like I was in a permanent "hunchback" state, as I physically curled my body to cover my broken heart. I would get anxious in groups and have scars on my hand from pinching myself to keep from crying at work meetings. And many times, I left grocery stores, coffee shops, and crowded events overwhelmed in tears.

And on both sides of fight-or-flight, we tend to reach for foods, drinks, shopping binges, or Netflix marathons to numb ourselves from the excruciating pain and discomfort that is grief, because it can be just too much to carry.

Many people believe that healing requires long retreats or vacations to escape our life and "reset." Of course, traveling to places that are grounding, calming, and rejuvenating can absolutely support you. In fact, travel often provides a zoomed out perspective of how big this world is, how many ways there are to live, and we can meet a lot of other people with stories too. It takes out the autopilot and any feelings of Groundhog Day. I love traveling.

But the deep work can be done through the monotonous and routine moments of any given day. And the more regularly we integrate healing work, particularly caring for our nervous system which is damaged throughout grief experiences, the better.

My advice is to keep it simple.

Nervous system regulation impacts all parts of our bodies, energy, clarity, and our thought process. We already explored how critical it is to allow our thoughts to propel us forward. But healing happens beyond the mind. Bessel van der Kolk, MD, published a book, *The Body Keeps the Score*, that explores this in much more depth. If you haven't read it, for now, just open up to understanding how our body will store emotions within, as if something happens, and the emotion or energy gets trapped inside. When you work on your nervous system regulation to remove yourself from the fight-or-flight response, you support yourself in thinking and acting more clearly. Not only is this supportive in any given moment, it prevents and controls subsequent damage that may result from acting from a dysregulated nervous system and making choices or having conversations that actually create more damage and pain in our relationships and lives.

When you are in fight-or-flight response, your body cannot heal; it is surviving. It is the body's natural physiological reaction to a perceived threat or danger. Grief, which shakes our sense of safety, identity, and understanding of the world, is a massive trigger for this. This response is controlled by the autonomic nervous system, specifically the sympathetic division of the autonomic nervous system. Everything in your body and mind is impacted.

Widely practiced strategies for supporting the nervous system, outside of therapy or coaching, include breathwork and meditation. I'll be honest, for me, these were not accessible for several years after losing Leyden. Breathwork triggered deeply the sound of Leyden's last breath, and meditation was often interrupted with racing thoughts that only increased my anxiety, because in that moment, I was then beating myself up for not being able to meditate correctly. While both have supported me over time, I do believe when something is challenging and triggering our trauma, it is often feedback that is exactly where we need to go to heal.

For me, there were three things that helped me tremendously:

1. Hot and cold therapy. Most commonly, this is through alternating between time in a sauna and in a cold plunge or ice bath. This actually physically puts your body in an uncomfortable state, and from being in it, we learn how to find calmness in extreme heat or cool temperatures. The first time I stepped into a cold plunge, I burst out into tears. I had no idea how much I was still carrying in my body, despite how much work I had done in my mind. Beyond the mental benefits of learning to stay calm when you want to scream, building patience, resilience, and more, the physical benefits support circulation, muscle recovery, and detoxifying the lymphatic system. For me, when I practice hot and cold therapy, it is a very individual, sacred, and private experience. I choose not to do this with conversation, friends, or from a place of adrenaline to see how long I can stay in the cold plunge. I allow it to be a spot where I observe my body and emotions, sit with what is coming up in the discomfort, and notice how my threshold for discomfort varies based on what is going on in my life.

2. Vow of silence. This is something I discovered on my own, and the benefits were astounding. I subsequently coached many of my clients to integrate it, and they, too, had incredible results. Think of how many words you speak out loud a day. Or how much your energy is going into other people or places. A vow of silence is a really simple way of harnessing our energy within. What happens when we do this is we create an environment of witnessing our emotions and thoughts in a deeper way than when we are interacting with others or consuming information from podcasts, music, social media, TV, and more. I also noticed that vows of silence calmed my nervous system by moving from a place of consuming and having my attention in so many places, to bringing it quietly within. When I take a vow of silence, not only do I not have conversations, I do not send voice notes, record any videos, or speak out loud in any form. Depending on your lifestyle, job, and family, this will look different for you. For me, coaching so many individuals, Friday afternoon and evening until Saturday for as long as I could proved to be the best time. If you have a spouse, roommate, or children, perhaps this is something you can even try together. In the beginning, even just a few intentional hours can go a long way. Over time, you can grow this to be a longer practice.

3. Scheduling in my grief. Even with the awareness, tools, and coaching, my fight-or-flight response wanted to stay the heck away from discomfort. I wanted to stay busy and distract myself from my reality. What I learned was that in order to make time for it, I literally needed to schedule it into my calendar. This didn't mean it was the only time for my grief; it meant that in addition to the daily waves and roller coaster of emotions, I was holding time each week to be with my grief. I might cry, work on a scrapbook, write about it, or simply lie down. But that time each week was in my calendar to make room for things to come up. One of my clients, Marcy, had been through a sexual assault that years later, she was learning to understand the grieving process to it. When we first started scheduling in time for her to "be with" her grief and pain, nothing happened. I explained to her that this is normal, and we are just chipping away to get to the buried emotions and layers. Then one day I got a message from her: "The flood gates opened! I cried for hours. I screamed! I feel like I just lost so much weight; I feel like a new human!" Sometimes we need to schedule in time and space for things and realize no immediate result may come through, but with consistency, it will have the room to surface, and only through it surfacing can we truly feel and then release it.

Strengthening the Scar Tissue

Think of what calms you. Perhaps revisit your toolbox and notice if being in nature, painting, cooking, or other activities you choose are ones that help you to feel more grounded.

Whatever modality you use, remember the interconnectedness of our minds and bodies and the toll that happens to our nervous systems when we are grieving.

Releasing Shame and Guilt

You do not have to carry this heaviness alone anymore. I am here with you, and I believe in you. Whether you are in fight-mode, flight-mode, or seeking escapes from the pain, you can do this. You are doing this because you are here. And that takes so much courage—to show up for you, your grief, and your future. When you do that, you are also showing up for your family, your friends, and your career because your ability to relate, contribute, and function in all those spaces relies on your ability to function as an individual.

I know, that seems brutally unfair. As if our world were turned upside down, and now we have to take responsibility for that? My heart truly wishes that wasn't the case. And my soul knows that by doing so, you will not only change your life, you will more deeply honor your loss and your story and more effectively connect and contribute to the ones you love. My entire life changed when grief taught me not only to surrender but to have support in place—strategies, tools, and new ways of training my mind and emotions.

I want you to remember this: you did not welcome grief in.

Any shame, guilt, or fear that you are experiencing is human, it's emotional, and it's normal. But I want to show you how to detach from that—because you have done nothing to have "deserved" this pain.

And I want you to remember this too: the suffocating pain of your grief will lighten. I don't believe in the illusion of a one-year finish line when things magically get better. This approach is not a seven-step playbook for you to move sequentially from stage one to seven seamlessly. Both the invisible finish line and the sequenced steps seek to have control and predictability in places that aren't controllable or predictable.

Believe me, I know. I tried all the things to beat, control, predict, and conquer grief. But it could be the most stubborn of all experiences and circumstances I have yet met.

And yes, employing action steps will help you, but the power is in knowing exactly what action step you need to take in any given moment rather than relying on a timeline and universal mold.

You do not fit into a universal mold.

Your grief does not either.

I want to share perhaps the scariest thing for me in "surrendering" to my grief in hopes that it helps you too. It wasn't the pain or even the recognition that I was going to have to feel deeply in order to get through.

It was the fear that by surrendering I was saying that I was "okay" with losing Leyden, that I gave up, or that I acknowledged that I invited grief in or was somehow deserving of this. I feared, deeply, that by accepting grief into my world, I was somehow accepting that I had done something for it to be there.

The fault, blame, shame, and guilt it came with made it impossible for me to emotionally breathe. As I learned, surrendering and accepting my grief was actually honoring Leyden and my loss. Grief was allowing me to heal productively. Grief was ceasing wasting energy in battling something that wasn't going to battle. Grief was placing energy on my own growth and transformation so that I could then give energy to others too.

The surrender was the courage.

The acceptance was the switch.

The release of shame was what set me free.

And you are not alone.

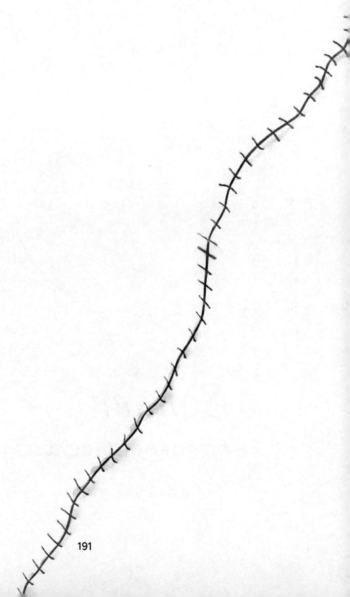

CHAPTER 15

Sonder

A PROFOUND REALIZATION

NOTE: This chapter provides more details on Leyden, and as such I chose to tell it solely as narrative without breaks. Leyden's life is a constant light, my ever-present Glimmer of Gold.

During the ninety-nine nights we spent at Boston Children's Hospital, at times, it felt like a vortex. Hours could pass in what felt like seconds. The sterile air, white walls, constant beeps, and intense emotions swirling from room to room made it hard to think or breathe. While it became my normal, friends and family reminded me that I needed to get out. It wasn't uncommon for me to spend days at Leyden's bedspace without seeing sunlight or life outside of the hospital. Knowing that my own mental and physical health would be better if I left the hospital walls, I became more intentional about doing so. As a former athlete, running became a coping mechanism that cleared my head, moved some energy, and allowed me to see the world that continued on around me.

Leyden's case was a roller coaster. We went in for a planned surgery, and unplanned, the day of the surgery, they adjusted because she was put on "NEC watch," meaning that if she had necrotizing enterocolitis (NEC), it would be too risky to complete the full heart repair. So instead of closing the holes in her heart, they put a band on the heart to constrict blood flow. We were told that this would suffice for a few years and then Leyden would come back to have her full heart repair. In the world of cardiac care, Leyden's case was considered to be "simple."

From surgery to feeding tube to NEC watch, back to surgery, and another and another, it felt like every day there were difficult decisions to be made or new information to process and understand. Leyden's father and I found that taking a short run down from the hospital to the Boston Public Garden, to process and then walk the garden while talking through our options or what we were both experiencing, was more supportive than trying to think and make decisions in the suffocating energy of the hospital environment.

The Boston Public Garden began to feel like a positive place where I did "mom things." My mom things might not include feeding my child, as she couldn't eat for much of her life, but rather zooming out from the emotions, considering what was best for my daughter, and also taking care of my own mental health so I could show up for her too.

I spent more time in the Garden than I may like to admit after Leyden passed. It was where I felt closest to her. It's also where I chose to spread her ashes. Our family had spent so much time in the Boston Public Garden—in between procedures or during difficult decisions—it truly felt like Leyden had found a home in that space. So with hands shaking and tears streaming down my face, I knew she was home. I had to remind myself to hold my breath as I poured out her ashes. At the time, it felt like saying goodbye—but in truth, I was letting her return to a place we had shared. After that day, I felt even more connected to the gardens.

I look back and wonder how I managed it.

Sometimes I really don't know how.

But isn't that the power of human nature? We have no idea what we can carry, and sometimes when we are carrying it, we don't even realize the weight of it until it's been lifted.

After Leyden died, I found myself returning to the Boston Public Garden as a way of connecting with the maternal energy that didn't have a place to be fully expressed or used. When I was ready to put some of Leyden's ashes into an urn necklace I had been given, I knew that the only place I was okay with risking her ashes being scattered in the transition was the Public Garden. I nestled by a small tree near the entrance, right by my church, and through tears and fear of the wind scattering her ashes, poured the remains of my daughter into the heart I would carry with me. Crying at my reality, I looked up at the tree, said a prayer, and slowly tilted the full urn of ashes into the necklace. Inevitably, some of the ashes scattered, and I quickly said that this tree would now be "Leyden's Tree." Many of the trees in the Boston Public Garden had memorial plaques on them. And although this one did, and was clearly dedicated to someone else, I decided that they wouldn't mind sharing with Leyden; she was sweet and adorable after all.

I shared the story of the tree with Team Leyden, and when my family and

I would go into the city, we would visit the tree. We even took photos in front of it, the tree with someone else's name plaque on it. I didn't care—the energy of what it meant to me was such a big part of my healing. Mother's Day, Leyden's birthday, and holidays, I would take a trip to the tree to spend time with Leyden. When there was a snowstorm on her birthday, I traced her initials and "HBD" in the snow in front of the barren trunk covered in white. My friend even had a beautiful long pink ribbon custom made with Leyden's name on it that I could hang on the tree on certain days to make it more "official." I can't count how many hours were spent there writing, people watching, crying, or just talking out loud to Leyden.

That's how I spent a lot of time, at the Boston Garden, just talking to my daughter. I felt like a mom again, close to my child even though she couldn't be with me physically. This was Leyden's space. Her spirit filled the garden, spreading light to help the trees grow. It was always there, beneath the same tree, that I felt closest to Leyden after she passed.

What started as a typical fall morning, heading out of my studio apartment in Beacon Hill, Boston, to go for a run on the river and end at Leyden's tree, quickly took a turn to a breakdown. As I approached her tree, I thought, I must be imagining this. I stopped my run and began walking. My eyes darted around the Public Garden to see if I had somehow found myself in the wrong spot.

I wasn't.

The tree was gone.

Only a stump remained.

I fell to my knees crying, buried my head in my hands, my body shaking.

Anger kicked in.

Feelings of injustice and my mind quickly went to, Why am I being punished? *You took my daughter, Universe, give me a f*cking tree!*

Before I knew it, my shaking fingers were tapping away on my phone, Googling the Boston Public Garden office, then dialing the number, barely able to catch my breath.

A woman answered. "Hello," she said, "this is Mary."

"Hi, my name is Melissa, and I am calling to find out what happened to a tree that was removed from the Public Garden. It's now just a stump."

"Oh my! Are you the owner of the tree?" she asked, confused.

I could hear her worry that the owner had not been notified of something.

"Well, no," I stuttered. "I'm not the owner, but that tree was very important to me."

She hesitated, clearly confused as to why a stranger was calling in hysterics to learn about a tree that she did not own.

Suddenly, my anger softened, and I was sobbing. My nose ran uncontrollably, my breath was still hard to find, the words stammered out between my lips explaining how I had "adopted" that tree. How I walked by it so many days while Leyden was in the hospital, my mind trying to get clear and figure out what decision to make, petrified of making the wrong ones. How our church was just in front of it, where her memorial service was, and one of the few places I felt safe in. And I continued on that when I poured my daughter's ashes into the urn necklace I wore each day, it symbolized being the place where I could be with her. And now, it is gone too.

As I heard myself babbling about a tree that I was infuriated about being removed, one that I had no right to call about, I thought, *This poor woman is going to think I am insane.*

Instead, Mary replied with love.

She explained that the tree was sick and had to be removed. She apologized for my pain and listened patiently as I continued to share how the garden meant so much to me through Leyden's life and loss.

She then went on to explain that I could get on the waitlist for another tree, but it would be a long time as they didn't plant new trees very often; already a long list of people were on that list waiting for their own tree.

In place of a tree, I could have a bench, she offered.

"Leyden was a baby!" I cried. "People can't sit on her like a bench. A bench would be for my grandfather," I said, "not my daughter."

Though I was aware that my emotions were spewing out in ways that weren't rational, I couldn't stop them.

To be honest, in a way it was a much-needed release. Having spent so much time in my mind, in learning, in the growth, I just needed to let it out. And I did as the tears only picked up their pace, and my cries loudened.

Mary, again, replied with compassion.

She asked for information and said that she would be in touch and wished me well.

I spent days thinking about how much like the passersby at Trader Joe's, frustrated that I was clogging the aisle, had no idea what I was carrying, or like I had no idea what the person who was weaving in and out of traffic in the jam-packed narrow lanes of Storrow Drive was carrying, Mary also had no idea what I was carrying. But her choice to respond with compassion, love, and patience, when she really didn't owe me anything, impacted me deeply—so much so that I recorded a podcast on it, wrote a blog on it, and still think about Mary often.

Months later, I was at lunch with a friend of mine right by Fenway Park.

We were eating at the same venue that we hosted the Leyden Cup at.

The Leyden Cup was an idea that came about with a lot of help from my entire Team. The doers, listeners, distractors...all made this not only one of my favorite days of the year but a tradition that felt so special and celebratory instead of heavy and sad.

We gathered in the downstairs of a local sports restaurant.

Leyden spent nine months in my belly on the sidelines of sporting events, got pep talks from me on surgery days, and when the "game" of the day at the hospital was to remove fluid from her wildly inflamed and swollen body, I made signs that said, "Win the day Leyden, get that fluid off!" I poured the amount of water the medical team had removed from her body into clear bottles and colored the liquid with the ink of markers from the family support center.

A celebration of her life and an event in her name was certainly going to involve athletics.

The Leyden Cup came about when I decided to run the Boston Marathon for Leyden.

The Boston Marathon is one of the most well-known sporting events in the world.

Runners gather from all around and compete to trek the 26.2 miles from Hopkinton, Massachusetts, to Boston.

As a kid growing up in Hopkinton, it was really the only "thing" we had each year. My small town did not allow chain restaurants or have a movie theater or shopping center. Riding our bikes downtown for Brigham's ice cream was about as exciting as it got—until marathon day.

Suddenly, our town turned into a melting pot for people of all nations and backgrounds. The street filled with vendors, and each year we would walk from my parents' house, a relatively short walk, to the starting line. As a kid, my elementary school hosted the top runners from the world who would come talk with us about possibility, perseverance, and how they often came from poverty-stricken homes and found a career in running.

The little girl who cheered on these runners, excitedly waiting to collect whatever clothing they shed at the starting line—sweatshirts and jackets that kept them warm, discarded for those cheering to take home as tokens of that year's race—had no idea what this race would mean one day.

If only she knew, while she smiled and enjoyed her fried dough, that decades later this race would represent the life, loss, and light of her daughter.

When Leyden was in the hospital, on Marathon Monday 2014, we were celebrating—celebrating the first marathon that continued forward a year after the devastating Boston Marathon bombing that shook our city and touched the world, celebrating the lives that had been lost, the bodies and hearts that had been injured, and the way the city united, even stronger, from such an attack.

And in the hospital, we were celebrating too.

Leyden was given a discharge date of that Friday.

We were going home.

In a moment of nostalgia, I took a video of Leyden, who was kicking, smiling, and looking healthy and bright.

"Say, 'Good morning, Uncle TJ!' Say, 'Good morning!' Say, 'We are stretching! Stretching our legs for the marathon!' Give uncle TJ that smileeee!" I sang as I danced my fingers up her belly to her nose. Leyden kicked her legs, darted her eyes, and responded with a massive smile. I continued in the video, "Yayyyy! Say, 'See you soon! See you soon!'"

Right after I took the video of Leyden stretching her legs for the marathon—in a moment of gratitude, pride for the city, and excitement to be going home—I looked at Leyden and said, "Leyden, next year we are going to cross that finish line for Boston Children's Hospital, together!"

It was soon after that Leyden met her Uncle TJ.

Just a couple of weeks later, she fell in love with her handsome uncle.

In fact, when he was there, she really had no interest in being with me; she just wanted her uncle to change, hold, and snuggle her.

Which he did.

But we were still in the hospital.

Despite having a discharge date of that Friday in April, we were delayed.

And would be delayed again.

And again.

And again.

Three subsequent surgeries, going on life support, coming off life support, and living (somehow) before finally taking her last breath in my arms in June of 2014—when we left the hospital, without Leyden.

The next time Uncle TJ and Leyden would be together was when he read the poem I wrote in front of a packed church at her memorial service.

Months after the service, I had found myself in a routine of rolling out of bed, reaching for the closest articles of clothing I could put on, surviving the day—maybe planning an occasional activity or dinner to distract myself, working where I could, and more often than not, trying to make it until 5 or 6 p.m. when I felt like it was acceptable to cut up some cheese, pour a glass of wine, sit in Leyden's rocker, and go through her pictures, videos, scrapbooks. Read the cards that had come in, look at her things, do anything that would help me feel close to my baby girl.

When scrolling on social media, I saw the posts that the applications for the Boston Marathon had opened. Boston Children's Hospital was accepting applicants.

Immediately, I began crying.

I had promised Leyden that we would cross that finish line together.

And she was gone.

I'm not exactly sure when it happened, but in the quiet and stillness of sitting in Leyden's rocker, meant to comfort her, now used to comfort me, it hit me.

I didn't make a conditional promise.

I didn't tell Leyden that only if I got the result that I wanted, would I honor my commitment to my word.

My stomach turned to razor blades.

I knew what I had to do.

I knew what I committed to doing.

And not even her passing would stop me from honoring my promise, as her mother, to my girl.

I was accepted on the Boston Children's Hospital marathon team, and part of my commitment was to raise money.

When brainstorming with my Teammates, we decided hosting the Leyden Cup, right next to Fenway Park, was the perfect option.

This cornhole tournament, silent auction, and raffle brought together around one hundred people—one hundred people who would read about Leyden's life on the posters I put out, who toasted to my girl, who formed relationships with one another, ones that they may not have ever created, if it weren't for Leyden. Seeing the love, laughter, and connection filled my heart with so much joy. This was a day I felt like Leyden's mom in a way that made my typically broken heart so full.

In addition to the annual fundraiser, I sent weekly emails. "Lessons from Leyden" filled the content of these, the very first spaces that I began sharing some of the deeper reflections Leyden's life, and loss, evoked from me—lessons I thought about every mile and step of the way as I ran that first Boston Marathon for Leyden. The 26.2 miles, unforgiving hills, moments of wanting to quit, and my body aching were a battle.

Remembering what Leyden had been through, the promise I made, and seeing the texts come in from my friends and family tracking me allowed my body to not only take on the course with strength but to have a better second half of the race, even over the infamous Heartbreak Hill.

Boston Marathon official photographers filled the course, and one of them captured me just before turning right on Hereford, before leaving on Boylston

Street to cross the finish line.

To most people, it probably looked like I was adjusting my sports bra.

But when I saw the photo, I gasped.

He captured me digging for the tiny silver heart I had run with against my heart for twenty-six miles, filled with Leyden's ashes.

When I crossed that finish line, my arm was extended over my head, holding Leyden's ashes.

Tears poured down my face.

We had crossed that finish line, just like I promised, for Boston Children's Hospital, together.

I looked up at the woman who put the medal around my neck and was crying so hard that my words, "I ran for my daughter Leyden!" translated to her responding, "Your father is so proud." Smiling, I took my medal and continued to walk the final few blocks to Leyden's tree where I met my friends and family, congregated in the church right by her tree, celebrated, laughed, and cried.

We did it.

It had been a few marathons later when I was on that run that knocked the wind out of me, discovering that Leyden's tree had now become a stump.

So it was only fitting that I was sitting having lunch with my friend at the very place the Leyden Cup was held, one of the friends I had also been with on Leyden's last day out of the hospital on our mom and baby coffee date, when Mary called.

Confused when I saw "Boston Public Garden" on the caller ID, I interrupted lunch to take the call.

"Melissa?" Mary asked.

I confirmed it was me and Mary continued, "You are not going to believe this. We had a meeting today, and the committee decided to plant four new trees in the Boston Public Garden. Four of them! Pink tulip trees! And they are right by where Leyden's tree was! Do you want me to reserve one for you?"

I had no idea how I was going to make the financial donation for this tree, but knowing there was no way I was not going to figure it out, I replied through tears, "Yes!"

The following year, as I ran another Boston Marathon for Leyden, I continued to the end of Boylston Street where Leyden's new tree—her official tree—the one with her own plaque on it stood, and this year, I tied my medal around it.

I have so many memories of that tree: moments alone, sacred; moments with friends sitting in beach chairs, having a picnic; moments singing "Happy Birthday" and lighting candles that stood in the dirt around the plaque with her name on it.

One of my favorites was dragging a ladder in with my family and covering it with lights, ornaments, and decorations for Christmas. To be clear, the tree decorating tradition we started was not normal. In fact, it garnered quite a bit of attention on social media, with people wondering why that one tree was randomly decorated. And as people learned the story, they continued to show the unmatched power of compassion and love. One year, I opened my phone to a message on Instagram from a stranger. She was apologizing, worried that she would upset me. But seeing that I was in California and seeing the Boston Public Garden staff cleaning the garden one day, months and months after Christmas passed, and the decorations remained, she went and personally took them all down to keep them safe for me.

A couple of years later, when my ten-day trip to Mexico turned into a permanent relocation, would mark the first year that I wasn't there to decorate Leyden's tree for the holidays. But it was one of my favorite years because that year, I was surprised by a FaceTime from Leyden's aunties, the same friends we spent our last day out of the hospital with enjoying coffee as new moms with many babies between us—who had all traveled from their different locations into the city and decorated Leyden's tree for me.

The power of compassion.

Love.

Teammates.

During the countless hours I spent at that tree, I found myself looking around wondering what stories other people were carrying.

No one walking by knew I was sitting at the memorial site of my deceased daughter—much like I had no idea what they were navigating.

There is beauty when we look at a human before us and wonder what scars are hiding under the surface, when we see them for the warriors they are without having to know a thing about them.

I discovered there was actually a term for this.

"Sonder" is a term that describes a profound realization that each passerby or person encountered in life has a life as vivid and complex as one's own, complete with their unique thoughts, emotions, experiences, and struggles. It's the understanding that every individual is the protagonist of their own story, living a life just as intricate and meaningful as one's own.

The word "sonder" was coined by John Koenig, the creator of *The Dictionary of Obscure Sorrows*, which is a collection of invented words to describe emotions and experiences that lack conventional terms.

Grief has a funny way of bringing things full circle. Months after Leyden passed, that same friend who I was sitting at lunch with when Mary called offered me tickets to see a well-known band play at Fenway Park—the place that now came to mark the home of the Leyden Cup, a major milestone for runners of the Boston Marathon, and the midway point exactly between where Leyden died at Boston Children's Hospital and where her legacy lived, in the Boston Public Garden.

It was incredibly thoughtful, and previous versions of me would have jumped to get to that concert. But what I found after Leyden died was that music, something I loved so very much, was triggering. My car rides were spent driving in silence, and if I did listen to something, it was generally a TED Talk or podcast around overcoming challenges or managing trauma. The thought of singing, dancing, and witnessing so much joy in life was overwhelming. I still didn't understand how the world seemed to continue on as if nothing had happened, when for me, nothing felt remotely right.

The first time I laughed and felt truly happy, I immediately felt guilty—as if I couldn't love Leyden and honor her and be happy at the same time. Eventually, I began to see that my happiness and choice to continue forward was honoring her. I'm not sure exactly when music reentered my world, but I do remember there was one artist in particular whose music was seemingly the only thing I could listen to for a period of time. The lyrics blended both hope and darkness. I was in awe of the depth of pain and heartache that entangled so effortlessly in hope and possibility. In a way, it mirrored everything the work I was doing in grief sought to achieve: to not "toxic positivity" our experiences but to feel them deeply, to know that they are passing and that we can continue forward. Upon researching the artist, Dermot Kennedy, I discovered that although he was based in Ireland, he spent a lot of his career playing in the streets of Boston. Boston has a dense Irish population and deep roots in the Irish community. Saint Patrick's Day in Boston is arguably the largest celebration of the holiday anywhere in the world.

Not only did I discover that he played in the streets of Boston, he actually played on the small bridge that lies in the heart of the Boston Public Garden, right near Leyden's tree. To me, he was the Tom Brady of music—an underdog who may have been overlooked early on in his career, but his resiliency, commitment, and relentlessness paved his path to becoming among the best at his craft.

As I watched his career progress and his transition from playing in the streets for free to filling stadiums internationally, I thought about the fight within him while he played right there, by Leyden's tree. I imagined him as one of those people I may have walked by without knowing his story. I empathize with the courage it took to show up day after day, to pursue a dream you believed in but didn't know how or when it could ever be a possibility—much like how I sat in that garden dreaming of the day my heart wouldn't hurt so badly, dreaming of being able to love life again but not knowing if and when it would be possible.

So while it was too soon for me to go to a concert at Fenway Park when my friend offered me tickets shortly after Leyden's passing, years later, when I saw a woman giving away a free ticket to Dermot Kennedy's show at a venue in Fenway Park, I knew if that ticket was still available, I had to go.

It was.

I flew from Mexico to Boston for just forty-eight hours to see him perform.

Standing just feet away from the musician, at the midway point between where Leyden had died and where her tree lived, dancing and singing at the top of my lungs, feeling true, sheer joy and gratitude as tears streamed down my face—it was possible.

Pain and heartache could coexist with gratitude and love.

I didn't "get over it," but I was moving through it.

Allowing myself to be shaped, not broken.

Allowing gold to fill my cracks.

And perhaps, to be an even more beautiful version of me.

Behind the singer was the name of the album and the tour that he was on: Sonder.

Aren't we all on our own sonder tour?

The protagonist in our own stories.

Running our own marathon, one step at a time.

Much like a marathon, the battles we are facing, the heartaches, losses, and grief we carry, do not get easier.

The Boston Marathon is still 26.2 miles.

Heartbreak Hill lining the course isn't any more forgiving.

But what happens over time is we learn how to train, how to prepare ourselves for the experiences.

We learn what our bodies need, when we need to push, when we need to rest.

We learn how to ask our Teammates to support us in ways that they can.

We receive unexpected support, energetic hugs, from strangers leading with compassion.

And we understand our own selves and needs at a deeper level than we ever have as we manage a course that feels like it can take us out at any moment.

And we remember that we are all interconnected. We all have stories.

Every single day, with the tools and the willingness to move forward, we get to write a new page in each chapter.

*Every single day I wonder what color
her hair would be.*

What her voice would sound like.

How I would homeschool her.

What arguments we would have.

What snuggles we would share.

What foods she would love.

What football team she would adore.

*I told my friend the other morning how
weird it is to know she "should" be alive
and also wonder if that's really the
highest power of truth.*

I don't know the answer.

I'm not supposed to.

*I believe my number one job (and
privilege) is to live, laugh, learn, love,
and do my best to share every single*

lesson Leyden continues to teach; to turn every ounce of grief and pain into more love, into creativity: writing, speaking, coaching, sharing, and learning. I'm constantly seeking new ways of transferring energy to serve.

So I can pour it into the world.

For Leyden.

This book is a means for helping me do just that.

Thank you for reading and for being here.

Of all the lessons she taught, this little six-pound sweet pea taught me what love is: the selflessness, spaciousness, timelessness, deep down to the soul, transformative, challenging, exciting, and makes you want to burst kind of love.

Afterword

Three Little Birds and Lessons from Leyden's Light

I sat in the car clenching the tiny little owl with giant eyes. Olivia was the name of Leyden's binky, the kind with the small stuffed animals attached to them. Leyden loved her binky. At times it seemed like the only thing that could bring her comfort when even snuggles in my arms and reassuring kisses couldn't ease her discomfort.

I was wearing the sundress I had picked up off my floor, wrinkled from wearing it the day before. It had become my grief uniform—one piece of clothing to put on, no thinking required when my brain felt like it stopped working, and it was loose at a time when I felt like I couldn't breathe. Tears streamed down my face as I stuttered, "I think I want to keep Olivia." Leyden's father and I were in the parking lot of the funeral home, dropping off a few pictures that would be burned alongside her body and the custom urns we had made with lyrics from her theme song, "Three Little Birds," adorning them.

The words of her theme song pierced my soul. We had chosen it on the way to the hospital when Leyden was going to be born. I believe everyone needs a theme song. You know, the song that you would play if you were walking up to the batter's box in a baseball game—the one that pumped you up, got you excited to perform, and you could listen to anytime you needed a little boost.

When Leyden was born, there were nineteen sets of eyes on her: my own cardiologists, her cardiologists, the NICU team, the CICU team, regular delivery personnel, and of course, the students from Harvard, who were just there to observe. Moments after she was born, every eye looked up to see what was happening when the song "Three Little Birds" was playing to welcome her into the world.

Now I was staring at the lyrics on the wooden urns waiting for her burned body to fill them.

And my entire world felt empty.

Olivia, Leyden's binky, oftentimes referred to as her "best friend," was in my hand, and I didn't want to let her go. After some debate and conversation, I concluded that Leyden needed her best friend with her. She deserved it.

In tears, I slowly walked into the musky funeral home.

I was surprised by what happened next.

Just days before, I ignored the worry about what the nurses would think of me crawling in to cradle my dead daughter's body, and I held her cool body against mine, pressed my face to hers, and apologized over and over.

The director of the funeral home said, "I prepared a viewing, if you would like. No one should ever lose their child."

Confused, I didn't know what was happening.

We weren't having a wake or a traditional funeral. Leyden wasn't being buried.

But he had created a viewing with Leyden lying in a tiny casket with her head propped up, wrapped in blankets. I couldn't believe it.

I got to see my baby again.

Thanking him repeatedly, I ran over to the casket and fell to my knees.

I pressed my face to hers, prayed, laughed, and cried.

This final goodbye reminded me that there is a beauty experienced in grief. The power of humans, of humanity, of kindness, compassion, and caring is unmatched.

And the gratitude that I felt is one I can still feel to this day. When we look at stages of grief and replace them with experiences and emotions rather than sequential stages, we can also expand those experiences to not only be filled with ones of pain.

Gratitude is an important part of grieving.

Some days the gratitude voice is quieter.

Others will speak more loudly.

And oftentimes, just like there can be unanticipated triggers, there can be unanticipated kindness, compassion, and love experienced.

I may have spent over a decade in classrooms, have a master's degree in education, and taught or coached thousands of individuals, but Leyden continues to be my most masterful teacher—grief, my most humbling and challenging classroom.

As a student of grief, I became a student of life.

Life teaches microlessons daily.

Grief just happens to scream at them.

It's less forgiving, less ignorable, and a powerful agent of change.

It can teach us to understand ourselves at a whole new level, to understand our Teammates and world in deeper ways. In doing so, it can actually strengthen and forge connections with others while also eliminating things in our life that are not working toward our highest good.

I hope that the hundreds of hours I spent trying to fight grief can serve you now. I hope the tools, resources, and stories in this book begin to lighten the load you are carrying in your grief journey. They have served hundreds of my clients and the thousands of people I have spoken to throughout the world. The way out isn't in winning but rather surrendering. Like a massive ocean wave that is crashing down, we are safest swimming with it rather than against it.

The truth is that life is far from cookie-cutter. In fact, it's the very bumps, bruises, and detours that comprise the experiences that shape us to be who we are and offer clarity in what we truly want to pursue. For us to find such meaning and clarity, we have to detach from the idea that things are supposed to look a certain way and refrain from the temptation of comparison, shaming ourselves, and fearing the perceptions, judgments, or thoughts of others.

It's a process; it doesn't happen overnight.

Grief reminds me of a marathon. I think of that first marathon I ran for Leyden and see a girl who was afraid to talk to anyone—who showed up to training runs with headphones on and head down while everyone else chatted music-free on the runs. But she kept showing up. Eventually, those headphones came out, and she became not only a captain of the team but a keynote speaker at multiple events fundraising for the hospital.

I think about when I was running that first marathon, and after persevering through what I thought was the worst part, I hit a tiny hill that was somehow taking me out—one I hadn't anticipated. And a man watching nearby saw my struggle. He squatted down enthusiastically, pointed both hands at me, and shouted, "You! You got this! One step at a time, come on, you got this!" I pulled so much from his energy to get me across my finisher medal.

Grief may not have a finish line. The journey of it will be filled with expected and unexpected challenges, with variables outside of your control, with times you want to give up and quit. But it will also have moments of light, of love, and learning and growth—of humbling lessons and of disbelief of the power of compassion and love from those along the route with you.

One step, one moment, one day at a time, you will continue to find the lessons and to find the healing.

And anytime you can amplify the voice of gratitude, without the cost of denying your emotions or toxic positivity, you will truly find more ease.

The best part? You are already doing it: you are already healing, growing, and transforming. And for that, I celebrate and honor your courage: the courage to read this book, the courage to open up, and the courage to pursue a life that is not one of survival but rather is filled with happiness, joy, and meaning—despite circumstances. The one that doesn't wait for things to get better to experience life but rather the one that experiences life and all aspects of it, through the pain, the messy, and the imperfections. The life that knows happiness can exist, even if the life feels unrecovered.

It is truly an honor to share this journey with you in whatever capacity that may be.

Thank you for allowing your heart to heal with me, to read these pages, and to allow my daughter Leyden's light to continue to shine far beyond her time here. Nothing means more to me, and for all that she has taught, and my ability to be a conduit of that, I am forever grateful.

With love and gratitude,
Melissa

Melissa and Leyden

Acknowledgments

To my parents and brothers, thank you for loving me and Leyden through all of it. Through the versions of me that were messy, lost, and broken. You celebrated me when no one else did, showed up in the moments I couldn't stop crying, and honored Leyden throughout her life and beyond. We even found laughs among the tears. You are the best uncles, nonny, and poppy I could ask for.

My extended family, from memorial gardens to tattoos to choosing me as a godmother and carrying on Leyden's name—I am so blessed to have you all. Thank you for how hard you have and continue to love both me and Leyden. She was spoiled with outfits, visits, and even more, spoiled with love.

Leyden's aunties—my college best friends and my "sister" Kait, from the days in the hospital, to the days planning her Memorial Service and every chapter after, you have seen, witnessed and supported me and are pillars for what it means to be a mother and a friend.

OG Team Leyden: the first email list of sharing Leyden's light, your marathon donations, the Leyden Cup turnout, and all the ways you so thoughtfully and authentically supported, you all deserve the Leyden Cup trophy.

To my grief counselor Kendra, my therapists, parent support groups, my Miles for Miracles Team who fought to save me... And the nurses and doctors who fought at Boston Children's Hospital to save my girl, thank you. Kendra, I don't think I would be here without you. You looked at me when I couldn't even see, broken in your office and said "Melissa, someday you are going to write a book that will change this world."

Mike Micahlowicz, for taking a chance on a raw and undiscovered writer. Mentoring me with wisdom and friendship; pushing me to see this book through when I wanted to quit and reminding me that the world needs Leyden's lessons. This book would not exist without you.

Penned to Purpose and Inspired Girl Publishing, the dream Team. I am so grateful for your care, intention and relentless efforts to bring this to life—even when I was avoidant, in pain, and wanted to shy away from "going deeper."

To my Team, thank you for the ways you are the most loyal, integrous, hard-working, and fun people to build a mission with. The days I needed to grieve, you managed. The time I needed for the book, you covered. The ways I struggled, you held. Thank you.

To my friend, colleague and teammate, Erik Rock, for spending hours with me to land on the title of "Scar Tissue" and challenging me to live the very lessons I was writing about, as I finished this book in arguably the most difficult chapter of my grief process, thank you. When you learned of Leyden, your conviction in my mission deepened and fueled my impact.

And to the readers holding this book in your hands, thank you for walking this path with me. I didn't write this because I had the answers. I wrote it because I wanted a space to be real. A space to heal. A space where we stop pretending and start becoming.

Thank you for being part of that.
Thank you for being here.

Acknowledgments

connect with Melissa